BIBLICAL STEWARDSHIP

BIBLICAL STEWARDSHIP

ALFRED MARTIN

EMMAUS
INTERNATIONAL

Biblical Stewardship

Alfred Martin

Published by:
  Emmaus International
  (ECS Ministries)
  PO Box 1028
  Dubuque, IA 52004-1028
  phone: (563) 585-2070
  email: info@emmausinternational.com
  website: EmmausInternational.com

Revised 2005 (AK '05), 2 UNITS
Reprinted 2010, 2014, 2018, 2019 (AK '05), 2 UNITS

ISBN 978-1-59387-040-9

Code: B-BS

All Scripture quotations, unless otherwise indicated, are taken from
the *New American Standard Bible®,* Copyright © 1960, 1962, 1968,
1971, 1973, 1975, 1977, 1995 by The Lockman Foundation. Used by
permission.

Printed in the United States of America

CONTENTS

♦ ♦ ♦

— ◆ ◆ ◆ —

The earth is the LORD's, and all it contains, the world, and those who dwell in it. For He has founded it upon the seas, and established it upon the rivers. —Psalm 24:1-2

For all these things the nations of the world eagerly seek; but your Father knows that you need these things. But seek His kingdom, and these things will be added to you.
—Luke 12:30-31

For what does it profit a man to gain the whole world, and forfeit his soul? For what will a man give in exchange for his soul? —Mark 8:36-37

Now this I say, he who sows sparingly will also reap sparingly, and he who sows bountifully will also reap bountifully. Each one must do just as he has purposed in his heart, not grudgingly or under compulsion, for God loves a cheerful giver.
—2 Corinthians 9:6-7

For all things come from You, and from Your hand we have given You. —1 Chronicles 29:14

But store up for yourselves treasures in heaven, where neither moth nor rust destroys, and where thieves do not break in or steal; for where your treasure is, there your heart will be also. —Matthew 6:20-21

For we must all appear before the judgment seat of Christ, so that each one may be recompensed for his deeds *in the body*, according to what he has done, whether good or bad.
—2 Corinthians 5:10

— ◆ ◆ ◆ —

INTRODUCTION

— ♦ ♦ ♦ —

If we ever had the idea that stewardship had to do only with money, this brief study of God's Word will show what a limited view this is, as there is no detail of life outside the circle of stewardship.

In a sense I am a steward whether I want to be or not, since it is a fact that I have nothing of my own. Everything has been received from God. But God wants me to be a conscious, willing steward—to receive everything from His hand thankfully, to acknowledge my complete dependence, and to return everything joyfully back to Him to His everlasting praise and glory.

Not my own! That is the essence of stewardship—to be conscious at all times that *all* I am and have is a sacred trust from God through the Lord Jesus Christ my Savior and to rejoice unreservedly in that consciousness.

One day we shall all stand before the Lord Jesus Christ to give an account of our stewardship. The efforts—and even the trials—of this present time will seem insignificant then in comparison to His approval.

> Therefore do not go on passing judgment before the time, but wait until the Lord comes who will both bring to light the things hidden in the darkness and disclose the motives

of men's hearts; and then each man's praise will come to him from God (1 Corinthians 4:5).

For we must all appear before the judgment seat of Christ, so that each one may be recompensed for his deeds in the body, according to what he has done, whether good or bad (2 Corinthians 5:10).

For not one of us lives for himself, and not one dies for himself; for if we live, we live for the Lord, or if we die, we die for the Lord; therefore, whether we live or die, we are the Lord's. . . . So then each one of us will give an account of himself to God (Romans 14:7-8, 12).

May we be like the apostle Paul, the great steward of the grace of God, who said:

I press on toward the goal for the prize of the upward call of God in Christ Jesus (Philippians 3:14).

CHAPTER 1

GOD'S OWNERSHIP THROUGH CREATION

◆ ◆ ◆

The subject of stewardship is much broader than generally believed. Most people think that it merely concerns what proportion of their money they decide to give to God. This approach completely overlooks the true basis of stewardship given in the Bible.

God the Holy Spirit says to Christians through the apostle Paul, "You are not your own" (1 Corinthians 6:19). In another passage Paul challenges his readers, "What do you have that you did not receive? And if you did receive it, why do you boast as if you had not received it?" (1 Corinthians 4:7).

If we really are to understand what stewardship is, we must discover what God tells us about it in His Word. We must begin where He begins and acknowledge that stewardship is, and must be, grounded in the very nature of God and of man.

GOD—CREATOR OF ALL THINGS

Space travel has made us conscious of the great expanses of the universe. Larger and more comprehensive telescopes have revealed countless galaxies studded with multitudes of stars beyond human computation.

What is the result of our expanding knowledge of the universe? As man discovers more about the universe, he is amazed at its immensity.

"How great it is!" he exclaims. This initial wonder, this overwhelming sense of awe, ought to lead to humility. Instead, it is soon transformed, because of the sinfulness of the human heart, into self-exalting pride. Because people's minds are blinded by Satan, "the god of this world" (2 Corinthians 4:4), they are overcome by false pride. "How great we are," they announce, "because we are finding out so much and because we are making such strides in conquering the vast reaches of space!"

What people ought to say, of course, is "How great God is, who created all these wonders!" This universe did not make itself. The Bible shows that observation of the starry heavens ought to lead people to acknowledge God as the creator. The psalmist sang, "The heavens are telling of the glory of God; and their expanse is declaring the work of His hands" (Psalm 19:1).

"In the beginning God created the heavens and the earth" (Genesis 1:1). This magnificent opening statement of the Bible declares the origin of things. True, it does not tell us all that we would like to know, but it does inform us that the answers are found in a person, the sovereign God.

GOD — OWNER OF ALL THINGS

Since God created all things, it follows that *all things belong to Him*. It is as simple as that, and this is the basis of all stewardship.

Abraham called God "Most High, Possessor of heaven and earth" (Genesis 14:22). What we call ownership among men is based on many legal considerations but, no matter how well-established the human claim may be, all property rights can be traced back ultimately to God. We shall see as we investigate this subject through the Scriptures that God's right of ownership is absolute.

Some passages that help us see the fact of God's ownership are these:

> For all the earth is Mine (Exodus 19:5).

> For every beast of the forest is Mine, the cattle on a thousand hills (Psalm 50:10).

The earth is the LORD's, and all it contains, the world, and those who dwell in it. For He has founded it upon the seas, and established it upon the rivers (Psalm 24:1-2).

"The silver is Mine and the gold is Mine," says the LORD of hosts (Haggai 2:8).

Worthy are You, our Lord and our God, to receive glory and honor and power; for You created all things, and because of Your will they existed and were created (Revelation 4:11).

Unless we understand His absolute ownership and see our relationship to Him as our owner, we cannot approach the subject of stewardship in a meaningful way.

Such an approach is entirely different from that of the usual man of the world. He thinks of God (if he thinks of Him at all) as someone to whom he may give something if he feels like it. God becomes for him merely an object of charity.

Does God have the right to do what He wants with what belongs to Him? Can anyone really question His right? Many do, but to their own loss and sorrow.

MAN'S DEPENDENCE ON GOD

It is usual for people to think of themselves as self-made and self-sufficient. Consequently, they regard everything they have as their own possession, as though anything they may give to God is given as a favor.

This philosophy is a vicious lie, originated by the devil and carried along by human beings' own sinfully inventive minds. No person can be self-contained; no one has any ground for pride. Basically, man has no rights. Just as we must ground our study of stewardship on who and what God is, so we must also base it on who and what man is.

Man is really just a creature—that is, a being created by someone else. The psalmist declared, "It is He who has made us, and not we ourselves" (Psalms 100:3). Man is really just a dependent being. He could not have brought himself into existence, nor could he last for an instant apart from the sustaining providence of God.

Daniel's accusation against the ungodly King Belshazzar was that "the God in whose hand are your life-breath and your ways, you have not glorified" (Daniel 5:23).

No human being can stop the inevitable process of dying, which is God's judgment on sin. Scripture declares: "Through one man sin entered into the world, and death through sin, and so death spread to all men, because all sinned" (Romans 5:12).

Man is helpless, though at times even in his unbelief he can put up a brave front. Nevertheless, the record is soon written of him, as of all the rest, "And he died." (For an interesting exercise, count how many times that phrase appears in Genesis chapter 5.)

Yes, man is a creature and a dependent being. It follows then that he is a *steward*, not an owner. The Bible is filled with reminders that everything we have has come from God. King David acknowledged, when the people brought gifts to the Lord in preparation for the future building of the temple, "All things come from You, and from Your hand we have given You" (1 Chronicles 29:14).

It is clear that we are nothing of ourselves and have nothing of our own. All we are and all we have we received from God; consequently, we and all our possessions belong to Him.

REDEMPTION AND STEWARDSHIP

The Bible tells us that people originally knew of their creation by God and of their responsibility to Him. In their sin, however, they turned away from their creator.

> For even though they knew God, they did not honor Him as God or give thanks, but they became futile in their speculations and their foolish heart was darkened (Romans 1:21).

This passage shows plainly that men are without excuse for their denial or neglect of God (Romans 1:20). Although they could know of His existence and the fact that He is God if they would only look around and see His handiwork, they prefer to glorify themselves and to enjoy God's creation without acknowledging that it is His. Then we see man worshiping idols which, because they are nothing, only serve to glorify man himself.

Idolatry leads to immorality and every kind of foul perversion of God's purpose for mankind. Because of this terrible downward course, all people by nature are under the settled "wrath of God" (Romans 1:18). The climax of this divine description of human depravity is horrifying:

> Although they know the ordinance of God, that those who practice such things are worthy of death, they not only do the same, but also give hearty approval to those who practice them (Romans 1:32).

Some may wonder what all this has to do with stewardship. The answer is that although man was created to glorify his maker, he fell from that original state in which God created him and is therefore failing completely in his stewardship. God commanded the first man, Adam, as he stood before his creator in innocence, to have dominion over the earth in subjection to God's will (Genesis 1:28). But something terrible happened. Man disobeyed God, and his God-given dominion was interrupted.

THE FALL OF MAN, AND STEWARDSHIP

In His infinite wisdom, God created human beings in His own image (Genesis 1:27). God had placed the man and woman He made into a wonderful environment called the Garden of Eden. Into the garden came the tempter, Satan, and Adam and Eve chose to disobey God (Genesis 3). In the simple but decisive test God gave them, they utterly failed. They thought of their own desires rather than the command of God, believing the devil's lie, "You will be like God" (Genesis 3:5). They followed the devil's evil suggestion and became not like God but like the devil, rebels against their gracious creator. This disobedience was the origin of human sin and it affected the entire human race.

Through one man sin entered into the world, and death through sin, and so death spread to all men, because all sinned (Romans 5:12).

This is only one of many passages in the Bible that show all men to be sinners. Adam became a sinner by sinning. We sin because we are sinners by nature, but the sin is ours and we are responsible for it. We have inherited that evil character which our first parent brought on himself and us (see Ephesians 2:3).

A NEW AND ADDED GROUND OF STEWARDSHIP

God would have been perfectly righteous if He had allowed all men to go into eternal punishment. He had a perfect right to do so. One of the basic truths we must learn, if we are to understand stewardship, is that men have no rights before God.

But God showed man mercy. At the very scene of Adam's rebellion and curse He gave a promise of a coming redeemer, identified as "the seed of the woman" (Genesis 3:15). The entire Old Testament is the record of God's merciful dealings with man in preparation for that coming one. The New Testament reveals that God has always had a righteous basis for forgiving sin. Peter wrote:

> Knowing that you were not redeemed with perishable things like silver or gold, from your futile way of life inherited from your forefathers, but with precious blood, as of a lamb unblemished and spotless, the blood of Christ. For He was foreknown before the foundation of the world, but has appeared in these last times for the sake of you (1 Peter 1:18-20).

Paul likewise showed that when Christ died He settled the sin question for all of those who lived during the Old Testament period as well as for those living after the cross:

> Being justified as a gift by His grace through the redemption which is in Christ Jesus; whom God displayed publicly as a propitiation in His blood through faith. This was to demonstrate His righteousness, because in the forbearance of God He passed over the sins previously committed; for

the demonstration, I say, of His righteousness at the present time, so that He would be just and the justifier of the one who has faith in Jesus (Romans 3:24-26).

These passages show that it is not human opinion, but God's revealed truth that from all eternity God had His lamb. The Son of God, the Lord Jesus Christ, came into this world at the appointed time to die for the sins of men.

Man belongs to God by right of creation but is in rebellion against his maker. Now man has been placed into a new relationship. *The death of Christ has put a new and even more pressing claim on him.*

This relationship, expressed by the word *redemption* or *redeemed* (to redeem means "to buy back"), brings to our attention a very important fact in connection with stewardship: we have been "bought with a price" (1 Corinthians 6:20), a price far greater than all the silver and gold of this transitory world. That price was the "precious blood of Christ" (1 Peter 1:19).

No man could redeem any other man, for all were under the same condemnation. The psalmist said:

> No man can by any means redeem his brother or give to God a ransom for him (Psalm 49:7).

Only the sinless, spotless lamb of God, the Lord Jesus Christ, could bear our sins in His own body on the cross (1 Peter 2:24) and could thereby take away sin by the sacrifice of Himself (Hebrews 9:26). He "did not come to be served, but to serve, and to give His life a ransom for many" (Mark 10:45).

Because the gospel of Christ offers a complete salvation, we can understand and fulfill the meaning of stewardship.

DOUBLY HIS

God has a double claim on mankind. Each of us belongs to God because He created us. We also belong to Him because He has redeemed us.

In many parts of the world, slavery was a common social institution for centuries. When the New Testament was written slavery was an accepted practice in the Roman empire. The slave had no legal rights. He belonged entirely to his owner, who had complete control of his person. He was not his own. At one time we were slaves of sin. The Lord Jesus said, "everyone who commits sin is the slave of sin" (John 8:34).

Paul reminded us:

> Do you not know that when you present yourselves to someone as slaves for obedience, you are slaves of the one whom you obey, either of sin resulting in death, or of obedience resulting in righteousness? (Romans 6:16)

Now we have a new master who has purchased us at infinite cost, having given His own life for us. We belong to Him completely and absolutely.

THE ESSENCE OF STEWARDSHIP

The most amazing part of this entire subject of stewardship is that God, who has this double claim on us through creation and redemption, does not want us to serve Him unwillingly, as if we had no choice. It is as though He says to the believer in the Lord Jesus Christ, "Yes, you are Mine because I made you; and doubly Mine because I have redeemed you; but I want you to be Mine because you want to be Mine."

Paul was supremely aware of this truth. He knew that God would not force him to surrender his life, but he delighted in calling himself "Paul, a bond-servant of Christ Jesus" (Romans 1:1).

God does not force anyone to be His slave. Rather, He wants us to respond to His love and grace by turning our lives over to Him, because in His infinite wisdom and love He is able to do more for us than we can possibly do for ourselves.

Chapter 2

THE MEANING OF STEWARDSHIP

◆ ◆ ◆

We have seen that stewardship is based on God's ownership by right of creation and redemption and that God seeks man's willing acknowledgment of His right. But what *is* stewardship?

The words *steward* and *stewardship* do not occur often in the Scriptures, but some of the passages in which they are found help us understand their meaning. Paul encouraged the Corinthians to:

> Let a man regard us in this manner, as servants of Christ and stewards of the mysteries of God. In this case, moreover, it is required of stewards that one be found trustworthy (1 Corinthians 4:1-2).

The apostle Peter commanded:

> As each one has received a special gift, employ it in serving one another as good stewards of the manifold grace of God (1 Peter 4:10).

Paul, again, wrote of his stewardship:

> For if I do this voluntarily, I have a reward; but if against my will, I have a stewardship entrusted to me (1 Corinthians 9:17).

Of this church I was made a minister according to the stewardship from God bestowed on me for your benefit, so that I might fully carry out the preaching of the word of God (Colossians 1:25).

The Greek word from which these words are translated has to do with a household. The noun meaning "stewardship" is the word from which the English word *economy* is derived. A steward is someone who manages someone else's household. A stewardship is the management or administration of someone else's household affairs. A steward is a trustee or agent for the benefit of the owner.

These terms are indeed appropriate for the Christian, who is administering property and matters that don't belong to him. All the property belongs to God and all the household affairs are His. The steward has been appointed by the owner and is accountable to Him for his stewardship.

The Lord Jesus Christ gave several parables about stewards that reinforce the ideas expressed in the Scripture about the need for faithfulness or loyalty. A steward needs many desirable characteristics. He should be wise and careful, for he must exercise his judgment in the management of the owner's funds and real estate.

Above everything else, however, he must be faithful. Faithfulness involves honesty, integrity, and complete loyalty to the owner. The steward must lay aside self-interest and think only of the welfare of the one whose property he is handling.

COMPLETE SURRENDER

In Romans 12:1 we read:

> Therefore I urge you, brethren, by the mercies of God, to present your bodies a living and holy sacrifice, acceptable to God, which is your spiritual service of worship.

The basis on which Paul makes this appeal to Christians is all that God has done for us in saving us through the work of the Lord Jesus at Calvary. Everything in the letter to the Romans has been building up to this plea. As believer-priests we have a sacrifice to make: the sacrifice of ourselves. We are not like the Old Testament priests who brought dying sacrifices. We are to *live* for Him who died for us (2 Corinthians 5:14-15).

If stewardship is to have any meaning at all, the believer in the Lord Jesus Christ must come to this point of surrender. Ideally one should turn over one's life to God at the moment of first accepting Christ. Apparently this is what Paul did when he asked, "What shall I do, Lord?" (Acts 22:10). In practice, however, many of us, through ignorance or lack of clear instruction, do not enter at once into this truth of *yieldedness*. Have *you* yielded your whole self to the Lord Jesus?

A LIVING SACRIFICE

What does it mean for me to present my body as a living sacrifice? It means that I give myself to God unreservedly, that I turn over the control of my life to Him.

Certainly, I ought to do this. I have seen that He has a double claim on me, the claims of creation and redemption. Yet I do this freely and without compulsion, fully aware of what I am doing. I do it with great thanksgiving for all He has done for me. I do it with complete trust that He in His infinite wisdom and love can and will do infinitely more for my good than I could possibly do for myself. I do it because His love has awakened in me a love for Him in return. "We love, because He first loved us" (1 John 4:19).

Why have I waited so long to do this? Why did I imagine that I could manage my life better than He could? This is the perversity of human nature, to rebel against that which is my reasonable service.

Now I am His—all that I am and all that I have. I am nothing, of course, and have nothing apart from His grace, but by His grace I have a life to live in service for Him. As Paul said:

> I have been crucified with Christ; and it is no longer I who live, but Christ lives in me; and the life which I now live in the flesh I live by faith in the Son of God, who loved me and gave Himself up for me (Galatians 2:20).

The love of Christ now controls me; like the apostle, I want to spend and be spent in the service of my Lord. Any property I have, as well as life itself, is seen in its true perspective as a sacred trust, a divine stewardship. God has put me in trust with some of what belongs to Him. Now I must live up to the standard He has set: "It is required of stewards that one be found trustworthy" (1 Corinthians 4:2).

CHAPTER 3

LEGAL OBLIGATION AND GRACE GIVING

♦ ♦ ♦

When the subject of stewardship comes up, some people think that all it relates to is "tithing." If everyone would tithe, they think, this would take care of the matter.

There is nothing wrong with tithing in itself, but the Scripture shows that Christian stewardship is a much broader subject than tithing and that there is a much higher standard of giving than the tithe.

THE TITHE: AN ACKNOWLEDGMENT

In Old Testament times men acknowledged God's ownership of their lives and property by the payment of a tithe—that is, one tenth—to Him. This system, of course, could be wrongly understood. One who did not realize the significance of it could mistakenly assume that the remaining nine-tenths was his own to do with as he pleased.

The payment of the tithe, however, was an *acknowledgement* that a person is responsible to God for *all* the possessions God has given him. In a very real sense God has entrusted him with all these things; that is, He has appointed him a steward.

The earliest mention of the tithe is in the story of Abraham and Melchizedek, who was king of Salem and priest of the Most High God (read Genesis 14). Melchizedek appears suddenly on the scene of history. We are told nothing about his ancestors. And just as abruptly, he disappears from the record. The New Testament explains that God had purposely designed the record in this way so that Melchizedek could be a *type* (a prophetic symbol) of the Lord Jesus Christ, who has an eternal royal priesthood, without a beginning or an end. Abraham recognized the office of Melchizedek and gave him a tithe of the spoils recovered from those who had captured Sodom and the other cities of the plain.

Hebrews 7:4 says, "Now observe how great this man was to whom Abraham the patriarch gave a tenth of the choicest spoils." Abraham paid the tithe to Melchizedek not because it belonged to Melchizedek but because he was the priest of God Most High, who is the true owner of man's possessions (Genesis 14:22). Melchizedek was God's representative here.

We next read of the tithe in the account of Jacob and his dream at Bethel. There he saw a ladder reaching to heaven, with angels ascending and descending, and he heard the voice of God blessing him. He promised God, "Of all that You give me I will surely give a tenth to You" (Genesis 28:22). Again we see the tithe as an acknowledgement of God's ownership and His rightful claim on all.

THE TITHE AND THE LAW

When God gave the law to Israel through Moses the tithe was included as an integral part of the legal system. The people of Israel were given clear instructions concerning the tithing of the produce of their fields, their livestock, and their other possessions. God's command was:

> Thus all the tithe of the land, of the seed of the land or of the fruit of the tree, is the LORD's; it is holy to the LORD. If therefore, a man wishes to redeem part of his tithe, he shall add to it one-fifth of it. For every tenth part of herd or flesh, whatever passes under the rod, the tenth one shall be holy to the LORD (Leviticus 27:30-32).

The tithe was not an offering in the strict sense of the term, but an obligation placed on everyone under the law; that is, if an Israelite were to keep the law, he did not decide whether he should pay the tithe or not. He *had* to pay the tithe or become a lawbreaker.

Various kinds of tithes were commanded by the law. The people were to pay tithes to the Levites for their service on behalf of God and the sanctuary.

> Behold, I have given all the tithe in Israel for an inheritance, in return for their service which they perform, the service of the tent meeting (Numbers 18:21).

The Levites in turn were to tithe their tithe:

> Moreover, you shall speak to the Levites and say to them, 'When you take from the sons of Israel the tithe which I have given you from them for your inheritance, then you shall present an offering from it to the LORD, a tithe of the tithe' (Numbers 18:26).

There was also a tithe for the feasts and sacrifices of the Lord, of which the offerer himself and his family took part.

> You shall surely tithe all the produce from what you sow, which comes out of the field every year. You shall eat in the presence of the LORD your God ... the tithe of your grain, your new wine, your oil, and the first born of your herd and your flock, in order that you may learn to fear the LORD your God always (Deuteronomy 14:22-23; see also verses 24-26).

In addition there was a tithe every third year to benefit the poor (Deuteronomy 14:28-29).

Anyone who thinks that Christian stewardship is just about tithing fails to understand the complexity of the legal system and to understand the difference between law and grace.

GIVING UNDER THE LAW

But even in the Old Testament the tithe was only a part of stewardship. The tithe, it is true, was an obligation on every Israelite, but godly Israelites gave offerings to God in addition to the tithes.

Then it shall come about that the place in which the LORD your God will choose for His name to dwell, there you shall bring all that I command you: your burnt offerings and your sacrifices, your tithes and the contributions of your hand, and all your choice votive offerings which you vow to the LORD (Deuteronomy 12:11).

It is clear from Old Testament history that many Israelites disobeyed God and did not bring the tithe. For this disobedience God brought various kinds of judgments on them. The prophet Haggai told the people of his day that they were not prospering because they had neglected the building of the Lord's house and its service (see Haggai 1:3-11). And the prophet Malachi accused the people of his day of robbing God.

"Will a man rob God? Yet you are robbing Me! But you say, 'How have we robbed You?' In tithes and offerings. You are cursed with a curse, for you are robbing Me, the whole nation of you! Bring the whole tithe into the storehouse, so that there may be food in My house, and test Me now in this," says the LORD of hosts, "if I will not open for you the windows of heaven and pour out for you a blessing until it overflows" (Malachi 3:8-10).

There is no commandment in the New Testament that says that the Christian must tithe. We can learn principles of stewardship from the Old Testament teachings, but the matter of giving for the believer in Christ in this present day of grace is not based on legal obligation.

We are not saying that the Christian may not tithe if he chooses to do so, but if he holds to the tithe as a legal duty he is misunderstanding the teaching of Scripture about grace, and he would have to pay the tithe before he could claim to "give" anything to God.

THE BELIEVER "NOT UNDER THE LAW"

Scripture plainly teaches that the believer in Christ is not under the law. "You are not under law but under grace" (Romans 6:14). This does not mean that the believer is to be lawless, but it does mean that the law given to Moses has no direct claim on him.

Many try to separate the law into parts, asserting that one part belongs to the Christian while another part does not. Scripture always recognizes the law as a unity. "For whoever keeps the whole law and yet stumbles in one point, he has become guilty of all" (James 2:10). The Christian, since he is not under the law, is not under obligation to tithe.

Some will argue that this is a radical or unscriptural idea. They maintain that tithing is binding on the Christian because God gave it before the law; tithing did not originate with the law. But the same could be said about circumcision. God gave circumcision to Abraham before the law. Like tithing, circumcision was incorporated into the law when God gave the law to Israel through Moses. Surely no one, in the light of Acts 15 and the letter to the Galatians (5:1-6), is going to say that Christians have to keep the ordinance of circumcision just because it is older than the law!

Paul showed that the believer is neither under the law, as the Jews were, nor lawless, as the Gentiles were, but in an entirely new relationship which he spoke of as "under the law of Christ" (1 Corinthians 9:21; "under Christ's law," NIV).

The believer has a new position under grace that is neither legalistic nor antinomian (meaning, against all forms of law). We have been building up to this truth, having seen God's claims on us because of creation and redemption. We need now to see how the relationship of grace affects our stewardship.

GRACE LIVING AND GRACE GIVING

The Christian is not subject to the mosaic system, nor should he be lawless in his conduct, but is personally subject to the Lord Jesus Christ Himself. Is it wrong, then, to tithe? Definitely not. On the other hand the New Testament does not command Christians to tithe.

If a believer decides in his own heart out of love for the Lord Jesus Christ that he will give a tenth of his earnings to the Lord, he is free to do so and will be blessed in it. But he must not do it as if tithing were a legal obligation, and he must not do it with the idea that the other nine-tenths are his own to do with as he pleases without consulting the Lord. Many Christians use the tithe as a convenient measuring stick, believing that they ought to be willing under grace to do at least as much as an Israelite was required to do under the law.

If the tithe is not binding on Christians, does this mean they are to be careless or random givers? Not if they are to please God. Obligatory tithing, especially if one tries to lay the obligation on another, is a form of legalism. But random, careless, occasional, giving is a form of antinomianism, and we have seen that the believer is not in either of these positions.

What then is to be the standard for a Christian under grace? The Bible lays down a number of principles for grace giving. In later chapters we shall examine these principles as they relate to the giving of money as well as to other aspects of life.

CHAPTER 4

THE FIRST ESSENTIAL IN GIVING

♦ ♦ ♦

The central passage in the New Testament on the subject of giving is found in 2 Corinthians 8 and 9. Let us now consider this important passage and several others.

A great project of Paul's third missionary journey was the collection for the saints at Jerusalem (see 1 Corinthians 16:1). When he wrote to the Corinthians about the part they were to have in this collection, Paul used the example of the churches of Macedonia to encourage and motivate the Corinthian believers.

The giving of the Macedonian Christians was a result, we are told, of the grace of God (2 Corinthians 8:1). Although they were poor in material things, they excelled in generosity and liberality (verse 2). They were like the poor widow who gave more than all the rest who cast money into the treasury of the Lord, even though her offering was only small copper coins. The Lord Jesus said her gift was more than the others because she gave all she had (Mark 12:41-44). Those who talk about giving the "widow's mite" when they contribute only a pittance out of a comfortable supply do not know what they are talking about, or worse still, are dishonoring God.

Many preachers of our day would be amazed if the congregation begged them to accept more of an offering than they could reasonably be expected to give. Yet such was the attitude of the Macedonian Christians in Paul's day.

Some church leaders today use emotional, unscriptural, and inappropriate methods in pressuring people to give money to the Lord's work. As a reaction against that, some sincere, godly ministers hesitate even to mention money from the pulpit. Yet the Bible says a lot about money and its place in the Lord's service.

If Christians can learn what the Bible says about this important subject, they will not have to be cajoled, threatened, browbeaten, or pressured into giving to the Lord. The Macedonians gave joyfully of their means because they had learned the first essential of Christian stewardship.

WHAT IS THE FIRST ESSENTIAL?

The first essential in Christian giving, and in all Christian stewardship, is the giving of self to the Lord. If one gives oneself to God, then it follows that everything one has belongs to God. But if one has not taken this first step, then naturally the next step will not be possible. As long as a believer considers his life his own there can be no real Christian stewardship.

We often say we have dedicated our lives to God, but we don't show it by our actions. The pocketbook or the wallet is a sort of acid test of the reality of our surrender. The Macedonians gave far beyond the expectation of the apostle toward the offering for the saints because they had first given themselves to the Lord.

> And this, not as we had expected, but they first gave themselves to the Lord and to us by the will of God (2 Corinthians 8:5).

In exhorting the Corinthians to follow this example, Paul reminded them of their superiority in other lines of Christian activity. In spite of their many failures and shortcomings, many of them did abound in faith and in the other virtues mentioned (v. 7).

Paul longed to see them excel "in this gracious work also." He identified giving to the Lord as "a grace"; giving becomes a reflection of what God has done for us. We are the recipients of *His* grace, and He creates in us a desire to be gracious also.

We should note that the apostle expressly said he was not commanding the Christians to give (v. 8). He encouraged them to follow the example of others who had done so much, and he suggested giving as a way to prove the sincerity of their love. They said that they loved the Lord Jesus Christ and their fellowmen; let them show their love in reality.

James used the withholding of material goods as an example of someone who does not have genuine faith:

> If a brother or sister is without clothing and in need of daily food, and one of you says to them, "Go in peace, be warmed and be filled," and yet you do not give them what is necessary for their body, what use is that? Even so faith, if it has no works, is dead, being by itself (James 2:15-17).

Scripture does not hesitate to say that the Christian's use of money is a test of the reality of his profession and of his love for the Lord Jesus.

CHRIST, THE SUPREME EXAMPLE OF GIVING

In this central passage on the subject of Christian stewardship, the Lord Jesus Christ is presented as the supreme example of giving.

> For you know the grace of our Lord Jesus Christ, that though He was rich, yet for your sake He became poor, so that you through His poverty might become rich (2 Corinthians 8:9).

Grace is God's favor shown toward those who deserve only His condemnation. It cannot be earned in any way. It can never be paid for. In Romans Paul clearly showed that grace and works are mutually exclusive:

> But if it is by grace, it is no longer on the basis of works, otherwise grace is no longer grace (Romans 11:6).

So how rich was the Lord Jesus? This question is almost unanswerable. To ask how rich the Lord Jesus was, is to ask in effect how rich God is, because the Lord Jesus Christ is God. Scripture plainly declares His deity. He is one of the persons of the eternal Godhead.

In the beginning was the Word, and the Word was with God, and the Word was God (John 1:1).

For He has rescued us from the domain of darkness, and transferred us to the kingdom of His beloved Son. . . . He is the image of the invisible God, the firstborn of all creation. For by Him all things were created . . . He is before all things, and in Him all things hold together (Colossians 1:13, 15-17).

We have seen that God is the creator and possessor of all things. The universe came into being at His word. Therefore, all this vast creation belongs to the Lord Jesus Christ, the Son of God, and is under His control.

God . . . in these last days has spoken to us in His Son, whom He appointed heir of all things, through whom also He made the world. And He is the radiance of His glory and the exact representation of His nature, and upholds all things by the word of His power. (Hebrews 1:1-3).

The Lord Jesus Christ was rich in being the possessor of heaven and earth, but He was also rich in other ways. God created not only the material universe that can be seen, but also an invisible creation which is without doubt far greater than what is visible. We read in the Bible of multitudes of holy heavenly beings who perform the service of God. These are ordinarily referred to as angels.

Angels are spirit beings, messengers, and servants of God, completely devoted to their creator and perfectly subject to His will. The writer to the Hebrews, quoting from Psalm 104:4 and Psalm 45:6, said:

And of the angels He says, "Who makes His angels winds, And His ministers a flame of fire." But of the Son He says, "Your throne, O God, is forever and ever, And the righteous scepter is the scepter of His kingdom" (Hebrews 1:7-8).

From the time they were created, the heavenly beings have worshiped and praised their sovereign God. Isaiah had a vision of the throne of God in which he saw the seraphim—"burning ones" or holy heavenly beings of a high order—around God's throne, ardent in their devotion, and calling out to one another:

Holy, Holy, Holy is the Lord of hosts, the whole earth is full of His glory! (Isaiah 6:3)

Speaking of Christ, John quoted from this passage in Isaiah and commented:

These things Isaiah said because he saw His glory, and he spoke of Him (John 12:41).

The passage is clear; it cannot be construed in any other way. It was the glory of the Lord Jesus that Isaiah saw when he saw the glory of God. It was the Lord Jesus whom the seraphim were worshiping.

On the night before His death, looking toward the accomplishment of His work on the cross, the Lord Jesus prayed:

Now, Father, glorify Me together with Yourself, with the glory which I had with You before the world was (John 17:5).

From the time they were created, the heavenly beings did not cease to worship, adore, and praise the Son of God. He was the recipient of honor and glory. It is difficult for us to realize the wonders and glories of heaven where the Lord Jesus Christ was rightfully the center of the attention of all the marvelous intelligences He had created. We are given only brief and partial glimpses in Scripture, but we can see enough to realize that "He was rich."

THE SUMMIT OF HIS RICHES

Although the Lord Jesus Christ is the owner of all things by right of creation and the object of worship of all the holy angels, His riches are vastly greater than this. The summit of His riches consist in the fact that, as one of the persons of the eternal Godhead, He is the object of infinite love, and He enjoys the bliss of infinite fellowship from all eternity. We cannot even begin to imagine the depths of perfect harmony among the persons of the Godhead—the Father, the Son, and the Holy Spirit—as They have always existed in all Their infinite perfection. God is one God, but He exists in three persons, and each of these persons is both the subject and the object of infinite love. We see something of this love expressed in the Scriptures.

For the Father loves the Son, and shows Him all things that He Himself is doing (John 5:20).

At the baptism of the Lord Jesus the voice of the Father was heard from heaven saying, "My beloved Son, in whom I am well pleased" (Matthew 3:17). As He said this to John the baptizer and others, He said directly to the Lord Jesus, "You are My beloved Son, in You I am well pleased" (Mark 1:11). Later, on the mountain of transfiguration, He said again, "This is My beloved Son, with whom I am well pleased; listen to Him!" (Matthew 17:5). The Father made clear His supreme and infinite love for His Son.

Because God is the only perfect and infinite being, His greatest love must necessarily and rightly be for Himself. This is not a selfish love, but a righteous love and mutual love shared among the three persons of the holy Trinity. This concept is almost incomprehensible to us but may enable us to see dimly how rich the Lord Jesus Christ really is.

Unless we have some recognition of His riches, we are unable to understand the extent and degree of His grace in becoming poor for our sakes.

CHAPTER 5

THE EXTENT OF CHRIST'S GRACE

♦ ♦ ♦

Our Lord Jesus Christ demonstrated His grace by—although He was rich—becoming poor for our sakes. We have seen how rich He was; now we will discover how poor He became. When we think about these things we come face to face with the amazing truth of the incarnation—the eternal Son of God became a man. A parallel passage to the text we are considering (2 Corinthians 8:9) is found in these words:

> Christ Jesus . . . although He existed in the form of God, did not regard equality with God a thing to be grasped, but emptied Himself, taking the form of a bond-servant, and being made in the likeness of men. Being found in appearance as a man, He humbled Himself by becoming obedient to the point of death, even death on a cross (Philippians 2:5-8).

We cannot understand with our finite minds how the same person can have two natures—can be both God and man—yet we know this is so because the Word of God teaches it. The Son of God, in becoming a human being, took on all the sinless limitations of humanity while at the same time never stopped being God.

The statement that "He existed in the form of God" indicates His eternal deity. The word *form* does not refer to just outward appearance but to the manifestation of essential inner being. There has often been controversy about just what the Lord Jesus laid aside in becoming man. The theory of some—that He gave up His deity—is impossible. God cannot stop being God, for eternity and immutability (never changing) are essential qualities of His being. The Lord Jesus Christ always has been God and always will be God. Nor could He give up the attributes (characteristics) of God, for the attributes make up His nature. God could not allow any facet of His being to be reduced or removed. We only have to study the earthly life and ministry of the Lord Jesus in the gospels to see Him demonstrating His deity on various occasions.

What did Christ lay aside? He emptied Himself of all self-interest. He laid aside the glory and honor that were rightfully His as one of the persons of the Godhead: He "did not regard equality with God a thing to be grasped." He did not consider being on an equal basis with God a thing to be seized or held onto.

OUR LORD'S SELF-HUMBLING

Why are we giving so much attention in a study of stewardship to the doctrinal truths of Christ's incarnation and death for us? The answer is found in the usual Scriptural practice of mingling doctrine with practical truth for Christian living. *Our stewardship is a result of His stewardship.* The Lord Jesus Christ is the supreme example of good stewardship.

Even though the Son always existed in the form of God, He took on Himself the form of a bondservant or bond-slave (Philippians 2:7). Again we see *form* is not mere appearance. He did not merely seem like a servant or act like a servant; He became a servant in the truest sense. We see an illustration of His servanthood in His washing of His disciples' feet on the night before His death (John 13:4-5). Showing His constant attitude, our Lord said:

> For even the Son of Man did not come to be served, but to serve, and to give His life a ransom for many (Mark 10:45).

It would seem that taking on human nature would be humbling enough for the Son of God, but we read further that "being found in appearance as a man, He humbled Himself by becoming obedient to the point of death, even death on a cross" (Philippians 2:8). Not a noble, honorable death in the eyes of the world, for Roman law reserved crucifixion for the lowest types of criminals who did not have the privilege of Roman citizenship. This death He endured for you and for me. "For your sake He became poor" (2 Corinthians 8:9).

But it was a victorious death. On the cross He exclaimed, "It is finished!" (John 19:30). He accomplished what He had come into the world to do.

HOW POOR DID HE BECOME?

Seeing the different ways in which the Lord Jesus became poor for us will help us understand better the extent of His grace.

We read in Scripture that the Lord Jesus was born into the world into poor circumstances. Mary His mother, and her husband Joseph, although they came from the royal line of David, were poor people. When the Lord Jesus was born in Bethlehem He was placed in a manger "because there was no room for them in the inn" (Luke 2:7). If Joseph and Mary had been wealthy, room could probably have been found, in spite of the terribly crowded conditions brought about by the taking of the census.

Their poverty is even more evident in the account of the presentation of the infant Jesus in the Temple forty days after His birth. His mother offered "a pair of turtledoves or two young pigeons." This was described as "a sacrifice according to what was said in the law of the Lord" (Luke 2:24). The usual offering set by the law was "a one year old lamb for a burnt offering and a young pigeon or a turtledove for a sin offering" (Leviticus 12:6). The offering that Mary brought was that provided in the law of Moses for the mother who could not afford a lamb (Leviticus 12:8).

As He grew to manhood the Lord Jesus has no earthly possessions of His own. We see the astounding paradox of the creator and possessor of heaven and earth walking about in this world with nothing. When He was asked about paying taxes to Caesar He asked someone else to produce a coin for Him to exhibit to enforce His teaching (Matthew 22:19). He said to a man who promised to follow Him:

> The foxes have holes and the birds of the air have nests, but the Son of Man has nowhere to lay His head (Matthew 8:20; see also Luke 9:58).

Homeless, and almost friendless, He walked along the dusty roads of Galilee and Judea, dependent—humanly speaking—on the material support provided by His faithful followers.

> Soon afterwards, He began going around from one city and village to another, proclaiming and preaching the kingdom of God. The twelve were with Him, and also some women who had been healed of evil spirits and sicknesses: Mary who was called Magdalene, from whom seven demons had gone out, and Joanna the wife of Chuza, Herod's steward, and Susanna, and many others who were contributing to their support out of their private means (Luke 8:1-3).

The Lord Jesus owned no real estate and left no property. When He was on the cross He evidently had nothing except the clothes He wore. The soldiers who crucified Him divided these garments, gambling for His seamless tunic (John 19:23-24; see also Matthew 27:35; Mark 15:24; Luke 23:34).

The Son of God did not come into the midst of worldly prestige, power, or wealth. His poverty was evident for all to see. No one could accuse Him of taking from the poor to enrich Himself. No, He became the poorest of the poor for our sakes.

Yet the physical and material poverty which the Lord Jesus assumed was only a minor part of the poverty referred to in 2 Corinthians 8:9. Many people have lived in poverty and in that condition have accomplished much and served their generation well.

Scripture does not place any undue emphasis on the fact that the Lord Jesus was poor in this sense, although it does draw to our attention the astounding contrast of His previous glory and His earthly condition.

But the object of worship of the angelic hosts also came into this world to endure the neglect and denial, and even the taunts and sneers, of men.

> He was despised and forsaken of men, a man of sorrows and acquainted with grief; and like one from whom men hide their face He was despised, and we did not esteem Him (Isaiah 53:3).

We can recall some of the horrible and untrue and blasphemous charges made against the Lord of Glory by evil-minded sinners:

> "Do we not say rightly that You are a Samaritan and have a demon?" (John 8:48)

> "Behold, a gluttonous man and a drunkard, a friend of tax collectors and sinners!" (Luke 7:34)

> "He is possessed by Beelzebul," and "He casts out the demons by the ruler of demons" (Mark 3:22).

Well might the writer to the Hebrews exhort us:

> For consider Him who has endured such hostility by sinners against Himself, so that you will not grow weary and lose heart (Hebrews 12:3).

No one was ever misunderstood more than the Lord Jesus!

> He was in the world, and the world was made through Him, and the world did not know Him. He came to His own, and those who were His own did not receive Him (John 1:10-11).

Even his own half-siblings (the children of Mary and Joseph) taunted Him about His ministry because they did not believe in Him (John 7:3-5). Some even "went out to take custody of Him; for they were saying, 'He has lost His senses'" (Mark 3:21).

HEAVENLY PRAISE AND EARTHLY HOWLS

The religious leaders and their followers became increasingly hostile and bitter against the Lord Jesus and progressively more cruel in their treatment of Him. Several times they took up stones to stone Him, but were unable to throw the stones "because His hour had not yet come" (John 7:30; see also John 8:20, 59; John 10:31-39). Eventually, the time did arrive for which He had come into the world. As the mob with their frenzied leaders stood before Pilate and he offered to release the Lord Jesus, they roared, "Not this Man, but Barabbas" (John 18:40). In response to Pilate's question "What then shall I do with Jesus who is called Christ?" they answered, "Crucify Him!" (Matthew 27:22).

He was beaten, He was spit upon, He was tormented; a crown of thorns was pressed into His brow; He was nailed hand and foot to a cross. And there before the gaze of all—with the disciples, for the most part, standing far off—He still endured the "hostility by sinners" (Hebrews 12:3). One can see the hateful priests and other religious leaders wagging their heads at him in gleeful malice as they cried:

> He saved others; He cannot save Himself. He is the King of Israel; let Him now come down from the cross, and we will believe in Him (Matthew 27:42).

> Commit yourself to the LORD; let Him deliver him; Let Him rescue him because He delights in him (Psalm 22:8).

This opposition is a part of the poverty of the Lord Jesus. We hear it in the contrasting sounds of the heavenly chorus and the earthly mob. "Holy, Holy, Holy, is the LORD of hosts," exclaimed the seraphim joyously and reverently as they beheld His glory (Isaiah 6:3; cf. John 12:41). "Glory to God in the highest," proclaimed the heavenly host on the night of Christ's birth (Luke 2:14). "Crucify Him, crucify Him," demanded the sinful human throng. What a difference was experienced by the Son of God, who had been rich and who became poor for our sakes!

THE DEPTH OF HIS POVERTY

What was the true depth of the poverty of the Lord Jesus? Far greater than what He suffered at the hands of sinful men was what He suffered at the hand of His heavenly Father. This suffering is expressed in the words of prophecy:

All of us like sheep have gone astray, each of us has turned to his own way; But the LORD has caused the iniquity of us all to fall on Him (Isaiah 53:6).

But the LORD was pleased to crush Him, putting Him to grief (Isaiah 53:10).

And the New Testament records the fulfillment of this prophecy:

He made Him who knew no sin to be sin on our behalf, so that we might become the righteousness of God in Him (2 Corinthians 5:21).

When our Lord prayed in the garden of Gethsemane the night before He went to the cross, He said, "My Father, if it is possible, let this cup pass from Me" (Matthew 26:39). Many have been perplexed about the meaning of these words. Some have even supposed that the Lord Jesus Christ was afraid to die, or that He was back-tracking on His commitment. This is unthinkable. Many brave people have faced death without flinching; could it be said of the Lord of glory that He was any less courageous? Could the Son of God renege on the plan the Godhead had devised to save mankind from sin?

What was this cup? Surely it was not death as such. Surely it was not merely the agony of physical suffering. But it *was* an experience that no one else could face. The Lord Jesus, who never had any personal experience of sin, was facing the prospect of being made an offering for sin. God was to judge Him for all the sin of the world, just as if it were His own. What must it have meant to a personally sinless person to be "made sin"? We cannot begin to imagine the agony of His holy soul. He recoiled from it.

But the Lord Jesus Christ did not stop with the plea, "Let this cup pass from Me." In fact, He prefaced the prayer with the conditional clause "Father, if You are willing." Then He went on immediately to say, "Yet not My will, but Yours be done" (Luke 22:42; cf. Matthew 26:39; Mark 14:36).

Later, when His enemies came to take Him, He asked, "the cup which the Father has given Me, shall I not drink it?" (John 18:11). With perfect and complete surrender to the Father's will—not a rebellious, grudging, regretful surrender, but a joyous willing surrender—the Lord Jesus Christ our Savior went resolutely to the cross, drinking to the dregs the cup of judgment from the hand of the righteous judge.

How poor did the Lord Jesus Christ become for our sakes? If we really want to know the depth of His poverty, then we must stand in faith at the foot of the cross on which He died. In that thick darkness we must listen to the agonizing cry, "My God, My God, why have You forsaken Me?" (Matthew 27:46).

Did God really forsake His Son as He hung on the cross? Not in every sense of the term, for Christ Himself is God, and we read that "God was in Christ reconciling the world to Himself, not counting their trespasses against them" (2 Corinthians 5:19). Also Christ Himself said, "Yet I am not alone, because the Father is with Me" (John 16:32). Yet there was a very true and deep sense in which God did forsake the Lord Jesus on the cross—as God the righteous judge, judging the sin of mankind.

God the holy one cannot condone or tolerate sin. He must judge it, or He would compromise His own character. Therefore God visited His wrath against sin on His own Son rather than on us who deserved it. At Calvary God forsook His own Son for you and me so that you and I need never be forsaken.

Earlier John the baptizer had pointed to Christ, exclaiming, "Behold, the Lamb of God who takes away the sin of the world!" (John 1:29). Quoting from the prophecy in Isaiah 53, the apostle Peter spoke of Christ's death:

> And He Himself bore our sins in His body on the cross, so that we might die to sin and live to righteousness; for by His wounds you were healed (1 Peter 2:24).

This is the depth of the poverty of the Lord Jesus: the holy Son of God, who from all eternity had experienced perfect and unbroken fellowship within the Godhead as the object of the Father's perfect love became the object of God's wrath for our sakes.

"Yet for your sake He became poor" (2 Corinthians 8:9). The death of the Lord Jesus Christ on the cross, as well as all the events leading up to it, was for the world of lost people. There was no selfishness in the purpose of the Lord Jesus in coming into the world.

> For God so loved the world, that He gave His only begotten Son, that whoever believes in Him shall not perish, but have eternal life (John 3:16).

The substitutionary death of the Lord Jesus is the heart of the gospel. To dismiss His death as only that of a martyr, to interpret it only as a wonderful example or moral influence for others, or to view it merely as an expression of God's hatred of sin, is to distort or deny the holy Scriptures.

Paul told of the compelling force of his own life:

> For the love of Christ controls us, having concluded this, that one died for all, therefore all died; and He died for all, so that they who live might no longer live for themselves, but for Him who died and rose again on their behalf (2 Corinthians 5:14-15).

As we are faced with the divine basis of our stewardship as Christians, may we respond in the same manner as the apostle Paul.

CHAPTER 6

THE RESULTS OF CHRIST'S POVERTY

◆ ◆ ◆

In considering 2 Corinthians 8 and 9 we have seen in some measure how rich the Lord Jesus was and how poor He became. Now we need to ask whether we are indeed rich, and if so, how rich we are.

Let us acknowledge that although God has not promised earthly riches to all His children, He has promised to supply our needs:

> I have been young, and now I am old; yet I have not seen the righteous forsaken, or his descendants begging bread (Psalm 37:25).

> Do not be anxious, then, saying "What shall we eat?" or "What shall we drink?" or "With what shall we clothe ourselves?" For all these things the Gentiles eagerly seek; for your heavenly Father knows that you need all these things. But seek first His kingdom and His righteousness; and all these things shall be added to you (Matthew 6:31-33).

There are other riches, however, besides those the world recognizes. The Lord Jesus solemnly asked:

> For what does it profit a man to gain the whole world, and forfeit his soul? For what will a man give in exchange for his soul? (Mark 8:36-37)

An individual's salvation is of more value than all the treasures of this world. No matter how large the amount of earthly riches, they cannot satisfy the soul's hunger, nor can they last. "How much did he leave?" was the question asked about a wealthy man who had died. "Everything" was the terse reply.

> For we have brought nothing into the world, so we cannot take anything out of it either (1 Timothy 6:7).

Consequently, the one who has salvation through the Lord Jesus Christ is infinitely rich. His riches are immeasurable and unending. Scripture speaks of the "riches of His grace" (Ephesians 1:7), of the "riches of His glory" (Ephesians 3:16), and of the "unfathomable riches of Christ" (Ephesians 3:8). These riches belong to the believer because he is in Christ. Paul set forth our position:

> The Spirit Himself testifies with our spirit that we are children of God, and if children, heirs also, heirs of God and fellow heirs with Christ, if indeed we suffer with Him so that we may also be glorified with Him (Romans 8:16-17).

What are some of these heavenly riches? Dr. Lewis Sperry Chafer in his book *Salvation* listed thirty-three possessions that are the believer's through the Lord Jesus, all of which are a part of salvation. Anyone paging through the New Testament can make a similar discovery. Salvation in all its parts is a perfect and magnificent whole; one who has even one of these possessions has all the rest, for they all form a perfect unity. The believer . . .

- is a child of God (John 1:12).
- is a partaker of the divine nature (2 Peter 1:4)
- has been translated out of the kingdom of darkness into the kingdom of the Son of God (Colossians 1:13).
- has new life in Christ (Romans 6:4, 11; 2 Corinthians 5:17).
- has been forgiven all trespasses for Jesus' sake (Colossians 2:13).
- has been justified in the sight of God (Romans 3:24; 5:1).
- is indwelt by the Holy Spirit (Romans 8:9).

- has received all spiritual blessings in heavenly places in Christ (Ephesians 1:3).
- has been sealed by the Spirit (Ephesians 4:30).
- has been baptized by the Spirit into the body of Christ (1 Corinthians 12:13).

. . . and is heir to many other marvelous possessions and positions!

THE FORGIVENESS OF SINS

If you know the Lord Jesus Christ as your Savior you are rich indeed, in that you have experienced the forgiveness of sins.

> In Him we have redemption through His blood, the forgiveness of our trespasses, according to the riches of His grace (Ephesians 1:7).

Christ has paid the penalty for our sin and died for the guilt of our sin. We can go free. God has freely forgiven us for Jesus' sake. The sinner has now been forgiven on the basis of Christ's shed blood.

The moment one believes on the Lord Jesus Christ, one's sins are forgiven, past, present and future. God says in His Word, "For I will forgive their iniquity, and their sin I will remember no more" (Jeremiah 31:34).

After experiencing God's forgiveness, King Hezekiah testified, "For You have cast all my sins behind Your back" (Isaiah 38:17). God assures His people in His Word, "I have wiped out your transgressions like a thick cloud and your sins like a heavy mist" (Isaiah 44:22).

The psalmist rejoiced, "As far as the east is from the west, so far has He removed our transgressions from us" (Psalm 103:12). Anyone who has received the forgiveness of sins through Jesus Christ is a partaker of the riches of heaven.

THE GIFT OF RIGHTEOUSNESS

When we consider the gift of righteousness, we should realize how rich we are in Christ.

How righteous do we have to be to get to heaven? People have many different answers to this question, but the only valid answer is that we have to be exactly as righteous as Jesus Christ. Nothing less will do, and nothing more is needed. This answer would drive us to despair were it not for the fact that God gives the righteousness of Christ to people as a free gift, which they receive by faith.

> He made Him who knew no sin to be sin on our behalf, so that we might become the righteousness of God in Him (2 Corinthians 5:21).

> For if by the transgression of the one, death reigned through the one, much more those who receive the abundance of grace and of the gift of righteousness will reign in life through the One, Jesus Christ. So then as through one transgression there resulted condemnation to all men, even so through one act of righteousness there resulted justification of life to all men (Romans 5:17-18).

This teaching is known theologically as the doctrine of double imputation. Our sin has been imputed (reckoned, credited) to Christ. It was reckoned to Him in the sense that He died for it as if it were His own, paying the penalty which we owed and deserved to pay. At the same time, when He died He put His righteousness to *our* account. This imputed righteousness is ours because we are in Christ. God can therefore justify us, or declare us righteous.

More than forgiving us, God has declared us righteous. Because He has united us to His beloved Son and sees us in Him, God can righteously declare us righteous.

> But now apart from the Law the righteousness of God has been manifested, being witnessed by the Law and the Prophets, even the righteousness of God through faith in Jesus Christ for all those who believe; for there is no distinction; for all have sinned and fall short of the glory of God, being justified as a gift by His grace through the redemption which is in Christ Jesus; whom God displayed publicly as a propitiation in His blood through faith. This was to demonstrate His righteousness, because in the forbearance of God He passed over the sins previously

committed; for the demonstration, I say, of His righteousness at the present time, so that He would be just and the justifier of the one who has faith in Jesus (Romans 3:21-26).

THE GIFT OF ETERNAL LIFE

Along with the forgiveness of sins and the imputation of righteousness, this wonderful salvation that we have in Christ—which makes us so rich—includes the gift of eternal life.

For God so loved the world that He gave His only begotten Son, that whoever believes in Him shall not perish, but have eternal life (John 3:16).

Eternal life is not merely endless existence. The Bible indicates that all people have endless existence, for there is no such thing as the annihilation of the human soul. The individual continues on forever, even though that existence is in separation from God in hell. Eternal life is that quality of life which God has and which He gives to those who accept His Son.

He who has the Son has the life; he who does not have the Son of God does not have the life (1 John 5:12).

"This is eternal life," said the Lord Jesus in His high-priestly prayer to the Father, "that they may know You, the only true God, and Jesus Christ whom You have sent" (John 17:3). The believer does not have to wait until he dies to receive eternal life. He has it now. The Lord Jesus said:

Truly, truly, I say to you, he who hears My word and believes Him who sent Me, has eternal life, and does not come into judgment, but has passed out of death into life (John 5:24).

Eternal life and the other gifts included in our salvation help us realize how rich we are in the Lord Jesus Christ. Through His poverty for our sakes we have become rich in Him. Since these riches came from Him, they belong to Him, and out of these riches we are to exercise our stewardship.

7

THE CHRISTIAN'S WILLING MIND

◆ ◆ ◆

Second Corinthians 8 and 9 tell us about the example of the stewardship of Macedonian Christians and, above all, the example of the Lord Jesus Christ in giving Himself for us. Paul exhorted the Corinthians to follow these examples, and that is also our responsibility.

No one is to be forced to give:

> For if the readiness is present, it is acceptable according to what a person has, not according to what he does not have (2 Corinthians 8:12).

Paul already knew that, a year earlier, the Corinthian Christians had said they were willing to contribute to the particular project he was discussing: the collection for the poor saints at Jerusalem (2 Corinthians 8:10). Note the emphasis on personal willingness. He used the phrase "there was the readiness to desire it" in 2 Corinthians 8:11. If Paul considered the tithe binding on Christians as a legal obligation he would hardly have used such language as this. We see in the sphere of money the same approach God uses in regard to our entire lives. He has a claim on us—a double claim in fact—but He prefers that we respond *willingly*. Therefore, He will not coerce or compel.

We see the principle of proportionate giving in 2 Corinthians 8:12: "It is acceptable according to what a person has, not according to what he does not have."

This principle is not merely a certain set percentage for all alike; it implies that the one who has more will be able to give not only a greater amount, but also a greater proportion, than the one who has little. The amount is not the essential thing in God's sight. Variations in amount are inconsequential to Him who holds the seas "in the hollow of His hand" (Isaiah 40:12).

The acceptability of a gift depends on the personal willingness of the giver. The one who has little of this world's goods cannot be expected to give as much as the one who is exceedingly wealthy. Experience shows that there are generous people and stingy people among both the rich and the poor. God looks on the heart (1 Samuel 16:7). He is not arbitrary, harsh, or unreasonable in what He expects His children to do.

The person who says, "I can't give very much to the Lord, so I won't give anything," has not learned the principle of the willing mind. When he does learn, he knows God does not keep books in the same way men do. Remember that the Lord Jesus said of the poor widow that she had given more than all the others who were casting their money into the treasury (Mark 12:41-44).

THE NEED TO BE HONORABLE

When the apostle Paul gathered money for the work of the Lord he was always careful to do things in the proper way. From what he wrote to the Corinthians it is clear that he did not handle the funds personally. That job was done by a group of men chosen by the various contributing churches, and a careful accounting was made so that no one could be suspected of using the money for personal gain.

> Taking precaution so that no one will discredit us in our administration of this generous gift; for we have regard for what is honorable, not only in the sight of the Lord, but also in the sight of men (2 Corinthians 8:20-21).

Titus and the others mentioned in the passage had the same unselfish attitude and the same earnest care as Paul that all things should be done decently and in order.

The use of gifts is another facet of stewardship. Not only is the individual believer a steward in giving, but officers of churches and other Christian organizations are stewards of God in receiving, administering, and spending funds that have been contributed to the Lord's work.

God will hold accountable a church or other Christian organization that is careless in its accounting methods, wastes funds that have been given sacrificially by God's people, uses money for purposes other than those designated by the donors, and generally fails in its stewardship. One Christian organization included in its prayer calendar that it might be as right in its accounting methods as in its doctrine. Such honesty is essential in doing the Lord's work with the Lord's blessing.

Money can be a great curse or a great blessing, depending on the use made of it. Wasteful use of the Lord's money can bring reproach on the cause of Christ and can hinder the effective stewardship of God's children by causing them to withhold all giving because some stewards have been unfaithful. One of the responsibilities of the Christian steward is to choose those agencies that will exalt Christ and will use the money properly for His glory.

THE NEED FOR MUTUAL ENCOURAGEMENT

Some Christians seem to resent anyone's talking to them about giving money for the Lord's work. They insist that the Holy Spirit is able to direct their giving without any help from others. Of course the Holy Spirit is able to do this. However these chapters in 2 Corinthians clearly teach and exhort Christians about giving money for the Lord's service.

Paul reminded the Corinthians of their zeal, which he had experienced on a previous occasion, and encouraged them to follow through, so that both they and he would not be embarrassed (2 Corinthians 9:1-5). There is no thought here of what we might call high-pressure methods, but there is clear authority for making needs known to Christians and for instructing them in their responsibility of stewardship.

One who gives such instruction is not depriving believers of anything, and certainly not defrauding them. Rather, he is helping them come to a place of greater blessing. Giving is referred to as a "gracious work" (2 Corinthians 8:7), but many Christians have not learned the truth of the statement of the Lord Jesus, "It is more blessed to give than to receive" (Acts 20:35).

We all need reminders from time to time. Even though we know the general principles of stewardship and are aware of our responsibility, we tend to forget or grow lax. "The world is too much with us," as the poet Wordsworth said.

Too often we are overly concerned with the financial struggle of daily living, and we forget the promise of our gracious heavenly Father to care for us and supply our needs. Thus we ought not to be offended when preachers remind us of our stewardship responsibilities. They too are stewards with a solemn obligation to instruct us. If they can point us to the Word of God and show us the blessings God has for those who do His will, they can give a good account of *their* stewardship.

SPARINGLY OR BOUNTIFULLY?

What many of us do not seem to realize is that the only thing we can really keep is what we give away to God. We hug our possessions to ourselves, thereby thinking we are gaining something, but time soon shows what fools we are. Christian stewardship is compared to sowing and reaping a crop:

> Now this I say, he who sows sparingly will also reap sparingly, and he who sows bountifully will also reap bountifully (2 Corinthians 9:6).

We all know in the natural realm that if we sow very little seed we should not expect a great harvest. A farmer who scatters only a small amount of seed sparingly in only a few places in his field need not be surprised if he goes hungry. God is trying to show us that the very same principle applies in Christian stewardship. The one who withholds from God cannot expect a great reward. The Macedonian Christians were very generous in their giving, even though by earthly standards most of them were poor people. God saw to it that they did not lose out.

Stewardship is an exercise of faith. Can we trust God for today and tomorrow, as well as for eternity? Paul, in writing to the Philippians thanking them for the gift they had sent him, told them he was thankful not only for what he had received, but also for what was being accrued to them through their giving.

> But I rejoiced in the Lord greatly, that now at last you have revived your concern for me; indeed, you were concerned before, but you lacked opportunity. . . . Not that I seek the gift itself, but I seek for the profit which increases to your account. . . . And my God will supply all your needs according to His riches in glory in Christ Jesus (Philippians 4:10, 17, 19).

God is perfectly able to supply all our needs under every circumstance. The point here, however, is that we need not fear because of our own personal needs to give to the Lord's work when He asks us to do so. God will provide for our needs if we put Him first. The question is one of values—earthly versus heavenly. Do we have enough faith to see that which is invisible, to realize that only what we give to God is ours for all eternity?

"EACH ONE . . . AS HE HAS PURPOSED IN HIS HEART"

In 2 Corinthians 9:7 we are given another principle of Christian stewardship:

> Each one must do just as he has purposed in his heart, not grudgingly or under compulsion, for God loves a cheerful giver.

Paul did not say, "Everyone must pay a tithe." He did not say, "Everyone is to give what he is obligated to give." No, the decision is left up to the individual believer. Some would think that God is placing His work on precarious ground in doing this. Not at all. He is not dependent on men; He has chosen to bless them by permitting them to have a part in His work of their own free will.

Therefore we have no right to tell other Christians what they ought to give. We can instruct others in the Word of God and its principles of Christian stewardship, but we cannot make the decision for another about the amount of his gift to God. It is "each one . . . as he has purposed in his heart." But this is not a natural heart. It is a redeemed heart, a heart renewed by the Spirit of God. David said: "Delight yourself in the LORD; and He will give you the desires of your heart" (Psalm 37:4).

God will not merely give a person what he desires but will also shape the very desires themselves. One who is yielded to God will desire, without compulsion or coercion, to do what God wants him to do. This paradox is inexplicable, but completely believable— because God makes it plain in His Word—that the one most completely subject to the will of God is the most free of all people. The principle is the same as we read here:

> Work out your salvation with fear and trembling; for it is God who is at work in you, both to will and to work for His good pleasure (Philippians 2:12-13).

A person who is yielded to God does not need to fear that he will not please the Lord. He can be safely trusted to make his own decision, because it is God working through him.

"NOT GRUDGINGLY OR UNDER COMPULSION"

Christian giving is up to the individual, and it should be marked by joyful willingness. If a man is cajoled or coerced into giving what he really does not want to give, he does not experience the personal blessing God wants him to have.

"Not grudgingly," 2 Corinthians 9:7 tells us. Christian stewardship is not a matter of "have to" or even of "ought to." It is a matter of "want to." We have no right to say to others, "You must give." Rather, we can say, "You have the great privilege of giving to the Lord, if you will." Christian workers have no right, and certainly no mandate from God, to browbeat others into giving to the Lord's work. "Not grudgingly" describes the personal attitude of the giver, the subjective side. "Or under compulsion" describes the objective side; no compulsion is to be laid on the individual. Anyone who tries to put other believers under the law is going contrary to the plain statement of the Word of God.

One of the tragic examples in Scripture of those who gave grudgingly is seen in the record of Ananais and Sapphira, who wanted to have a reputation for giving all while they withheld part from God. Peter said:

> "While it remained unsold, did it not remain your own? And after it was sold, was it not under your control? Why is it that you have conceived this deed in your heart? You have not lied to men but to God" (Acts 5:4).

A wonderful example, on the other hand, of ungrudging giving is seen in the time of David:

> Then the people rejoiced because they had offered so willingly, for they made their offering to the LORD with a whole heart, and King David also rejoiced greatly (1 Chronicles 29:9).

David's prayer at this time is also instructive:

> For all things come from You, and from Your hand we have given You (1 Chronicles 29:14).

When a Christian learns to give "not grudgingly or under compulsion," he experiences that liberty which is the gift of the Holy Spirit. Stewardship becomes a joyous privilege, not an irritating duty.

"A CHEERFUL GIVER"

"God loves a cheerful giver" (2 Corinthians 9:7). This declaration raises a question. Does not God love everyone? Yes, we know that God loves all people; the proof of this is in His giving His Son to die for the sins of the world.

But God demonstrates His own love toward us, in that while we were yet sinners, Christ died for us (Romans 5:8).

Scripture teaches, however, that God has a special love for those who know and belong to the Lord Jesus, who said:

> "He who has My commandments and keeps them is the one who loves Me; and he who loves Me will be loved by My Father, and I will love him and will disclose Myself to him. . . . If anyone loves Me, he will keep My word; and My Father will love him, and We will come to him and make Our abode with him" (John 14:21, 23).

God has a special love toward the cheerful giver. Such a giver puts God first and recognizes that His cause takes precedence over every other claim, even the most legitimate. His heart overflows with gratitude to God who has done so much for us.

Shakespeare's King Lear exclaimed, "How sharper than a serpent's tooth it is to have a thankless child." Sad to say, God has many thankless children. But the one who has been taught by the Holy Spirit the enormity of his lost condition, the horror of the pit from which he has been rescued, and the magnitude and perfection of salvation through Christ, responds joyfully.

The joy of the Lord reaches the pocketbook. It causes what, under other conditions, would be so jealously guarded for self-satisfaction to be poured forth freely for the honor of Christ, just as Mary of Bethany poured out the "costly perfume of pure nard" on His feet (John 12:3; cf. Matthew 26:7; Mark 14:3).

The cheerful giver is like the Macedonian believers:

> That in a great ordeal of affliction their abundance of joy and their deep poverty overflowed in the wealth of their liberality . . . begging us with much urging for the favor of participation in the support of the saints (2 Corinthians 8:2, 4).

The one who gives without compunction or inner restraint is like God Himself, who did not withhold His greatest treasure but willingly offered up His beloved Son for lost mankind.

He who did not spare His own Son, but delivered Him over for us all, how will He not also with Him freely give us all things? (Romans 8:32)

"ALL SUFFICIENCY IN EVERYTHING"

In contrast to the cheerful giver is the Christian who says he would like to give to the Lord's work but hesitates because he is afraid he will not have enough for himself. This one has forgotten that no one can out-give God. He realizes, of course, that God will guide him to provide for his household (see 1 Timothy 5:8), to pay his debts fully and promptly, and not to shirk any legitimate obligation toward any man. To refuse to pay just debts on the grounds that the money is to be given to the service of Christ is to dishonor the Lord.

If we obey joyfully the call of the Spirit of God concerning our Christian stewardship, can we doubt that our heavenly Father will provide for us?

> And God is able to make all grace abound to you, so that always having all sufficiency in everything, you may have an abundance for every good deed (2 Corinthians 9:8).

It is an eternal principle that God will be no man's debtor. The one who gives to God will receive back in full measure, and much more besides. "Test me now in this," God challenged Israel, "if I will not . . . pour out for you a blessing until it overflows" (Malachi 3:10). Can we afford to give to God? The Lord Jesus said,

> "Give, and it will be given to you. They will pour into your lap a good measure—pressed down, shaken together, and running over. For by your standard of measure it will be measured to you in return" (Luke 6:38).

> "Truly I say to you, there is no one who has left house or wife or brothers or parents or children, for the sake of the kingdom of God, who will not receive many times as much at this time and in the age to come, eternal life" (Luke 18:29-30).

The true motive in giving is not to receive something in return; it is love toward God. Giving merely in order to get is not really giving;

it is just a means of getting. Nevertheless one cannot give to God without getting something in return. That is the nature of God.

GREATER GLORY TO GOD

As 2 Corinthians 9:9-14 shows, the willing, cheerful giving of God's people to His cause brings greater glory to Him through the thanksgiving of many who are helped. Who can calculate the effect of a dollar given prayerfully to buy tracts through which some learn of Christ and accept Him? Or money given for the support of a pioneer missionary in some far-off land, who brings the word of life to those who sit in darkness? Or funds designated for the training of some of God's choice young servants, that they might be equipped and prepared to take the gospel of Christ to the end of the earth?

If God will not forget, but will honor, the cup of cold water given "in the name of a disciple" (Matthew 10:42), we can be assured that nothing truly given to God will ever be wasted. Like a great revolving fund, our small part, given with gratitude and prayer, will keep on working for the Lord. The effect on a life of a simple gospel tract may cause that life to be fruitful in reaching other lives who in turn may reach out to others. The consequences go on and on for God's glory, and in heaven many will have cause to rejoice and to thank Him even for the little that we gave. Yes, God will multiply the "seed" we sow (2 Corinthians 9:10). The God who could feed the 5,000 with five loaves and two fish can also perform miracles with our pittance.

Our failing is that we, like Israel of old, limit God (see Psalm 78:41). It is recorded of our Lord Jesus that in Nazareth He "did not do many miracles there because of their unbelief" (Matthew 13:58). We need an effervescent faith, welling up from deep within through the power of the Holy Spirit, enabling us to give without counting the cost for Christ's sake, and resulting in greater glory to God.

"HIS INDESCRIBABLE GIFT"

This section on Christian stewardship (2 Corinthians 8 and 9) is brought to a close and a climax by the exclamation of the apostle: "Thanks be to God for His indescribable gift!" (2 Corinthians 9:15).

The free gift of God is *indescribable*, referring in the original text to that which cannot be put into words. The English word *unspeakable* of the King James Version has changed in meaning since 1611 and is no longer appropriate. Language is inadequate to describe all the Lord Jesus is in His person and His work, but Scripture tells us that "His name will be called Wonderful" (Isaiah 9:6).

He is wonderful in His person. There is no one else like the Lord Jesus Christ. He is the unique one, the Son of God and Son of Man (1 Timothy 3:16). He is the holy one, the loving one, the merciful one, and the compassionate one. He "went about doing good and healing all who were oppressed by the devil" (Acts 10:38).

He is wonderful in His work. No one else could do what the Lord Jesus did. The psalmist said of all mankind, "No man can by any means redeem his brother or give to God a ransom for him" (Psalm 49:7). But the Lord Jesus Christ could, and did, redeem. "When He had made purification of sins, He sat down at the right hand of the Majesty on high" (Hebrews 1:3).

What more can we say except to join with the apostle in exclaiming, "Thanks be to God for His indescribable gift!"

8

MONEY—FOR SELF OR FOR GOD?

♦ ♦ ♦

We shall now look briefly at some other Scripture portions dealing with the Christian stewardship of money.

SYSTEMATIC GIVING

Paul brings to our notice the principle of regularity in giving to the Lord.

> Now concerning the collection for the saints, as I directed the churches of Galatia, so do you also. On the first day of every week each one of you is to put aside and save, as he may prosper, so that no collections be made when I come (1 Corinthians 16:1-2).

Paul showed that the regular setting aside of money for the Lord's work is preferable to sporadic or infrequent drives for money. Each believer, in careful recognition of God's bounty to him, is to set aside regularly what he believes God would have him give to Him.

The first day of the week was specifically mentioned because this is the day believers meet together in memory of the Lord Jesus, to worship Him, to fellowship in spiritual things, and to be taught from His Word. Is it not fitting then that the believer should make giving a vital part of his worship and service?

The believer should give "as he may prosper." This prosperity comes from God, not because God owes it to us, but out of His free love and grace. All good things come from God.

> Every good thing given and every perfect gift is from above, coming down from the Father of lights, with whom there is no variation or shifting shadow (James 1:17).

"BUT ISN'T MONEY EVIL?"

Some people will object to Christians talking so much about money. After all, some ask, doesn't Scripture say that money is evil? How, then, can money be used to glorify God?

There are several places in the King James Version in which the term *filthy lucre* is used for money (1 Timothy 3:3, 8; Titus 1:7, 11; 1 Peter 5:2). In Greek (the language the New Testament was written in) the word used in 1 Timothy 3:3 means literally "not loving money" or "not avaricious." In the passage just cited, the New King James Version (NKJV) translates it as "not greedy for money." The other occurrence is in Hebrews 13:5, where NKJV translates it as "without covetousness."

A different word is used in 1 Timothy 3:8, where NKJV translates it as "not greedy for money," since this verse is similar to 1 Timothy 3:3, although not identical. The same adjective form is used in Titus 1:7, where NKJV renders it as "not greedy for money" and the New American Standard Bible (NASB) translates it as "not fond of sordid gain." The same root is used adverbially in 1 Peter 5:2, where NASB translates it as "sordid gain."

One can readily see from these passages that it is the *motive* of the person involved and his use of money that makes money "filthy" or "sordid." The officer of the church who performs his service only for personal gain thereby causes the money that he receives to become "filthy" or "sordid" in God's reckoning. There is nothing good or bad, moral or immoral, about money as such. The moral quality is given to money by our attitude toward it and the uses we make of it.

The Lord Jesus solemnly warned:

No one can serve two masters; for either he will hate the one and love the other, or he will be devoted to one and despise the other. You cannot serve God and wealth (Matthew 6:24; cf. Luke 16:13).

Here are two utterly contrasting principles for living. Is the believer to be a servant of God or a servant of money? (*Mammon* is an Aramaic word referring to money or riches.) Money ought to be a servant or a tool; man should not to be a slave to money. Too many people, however, have become enslaved to their own covetousness and have consequently failed to serve God. "You cannot serve God and wealth."

"THE LOVE OF MONEY"

God does not say that money is evil. We read in 1 Timothy 6:10 that "the love of money is a root of all sorts of evil." The sin of covetousness (greedy desire) is sometimes linked in Scripture as being just as wicked as gross sins of immorality (see Mark 7:21-23 and 1 Corinthians 6:9-10). Paul spoke of "greed, which amounts to idolatry" (Colossians 3:5) and reminded us that some of the Lord's disciples have so coveted money that they "have wandered away from the faith and pierced themselves with many griefs" (1 Timothy 6:10).

> But those who want to get rich fall into temptation and a snare and many foolish and harmful desires which plunge men into ruin and destruction (1 Timothy 6:9).

Paul did not mean that poor people are better than rich people, or that riches are sinful; he did mean that wealth brings temptations into a person's life that may cause him to forget his obligations to God.

Riches cannot be trusted. They cannot bring lasting satisfaction. Solomon painted a graphic picture of the rich man who lacks the health to enjoy his riches:

> There is an evil which I have seen under the sun and it is prevalent among men—a man to whom God has given riches and wealth and honor so that his soul lacks nothing of all

that he desires; yet God has not empowered him to eat from them, for a foreigner enjoys them. This is vanity and a severe affliction (Ecclesiastes 6:1-2).

Christians are charged not "to fix their hope on the uncertainty of riches, but on God, who richly supplies us with all things to enjoy" (1 Timothy 6:17). We can make use of the money God has given us. As a steward of God's bounty we should spend it in the right way, not heaping up treasures here on earth, but following these instructions:

> Instruct them to do good, to be rich in good works, to be generous and ready to share, storing up for themselves the treasure of a good foundation for the future, so that they may take hold of that which is life indeed (1 Timothy 6:18-19).

Only what we give to God will be ours throughout all eternity.

MAKING FRIENDS BY MEANS OF UNRIGHTEOUS WEALTH

Other principles of stewardship are found in the parable of the unjust steward as given by the Lord Jesus:

> There was a rich man who had a manager, and this manager was reported to him as squandering his possessions. And he called him and said to him, "What is this I hear about you? Give an accounting of your management, for you can no longer be manager." The manager said to himself, "What shall I do, since my master is taking the management away from me? I am not strong enough to dig; I am ashamed to beg. I know what I shall do, so that when I am removed from the management people will welcome me into their homes." And he summoned each one of his master's debtors, and he began saying to the first, "How much do you owe my master?" And he said, "A hundred measures of oil." And he said to him, "Take your bill, and sit down quickly and write fifty." Then he said to another, "And how much do you owe?" And he said, "A hundred measures of wheat." And he said to him, "Take your bill, and write eighty." And

his master praised the unrighteous manager because he had acted shrewdly; for the sons of this age are more shrewd in relation to their own kind than the sons of light. And I say to you, make friends for yourselves by means of the wealth of unrighteousness, so that when it fails, they will receive you into the eternal dwellings. He who is faithful in a very little thing is faithful also in much; and he who is unrighteous in a very little thing is unrighteous also in much. Therefore if you have not been faithful in the use of unrighteous wealth, who will entrust the true riches to you? And if you have not been faithful in the use of that which is another's, who will give you that which is your own? (Luke 16:1-12)

Our Lord does not commend the steward in this parable for his actions; it was his human master—*that* lord—who commended him, because he evidently admired what we might call his gall or "brass." The Lord Jesus commented, "The sons of this age are more shrewd in relation to their own kind than the sons of light" (Luke 16:8).

What the steward did was technically legal because he had been entrusted with the control of his master's property. He discounted the debts that were owed to his master, not only liquidating those frozen assets but at the same time making friends of those whose debts he had reduced.

The Lord Jesus pointed out how the steward had *unrighteously* used for his own advantage the funds entrusted to him. We, as His stewards, should *righteously* use for our own advantage the funds entrusted to us (look again at Luke 16:9). Whatever wealth we have is a part of the unrighteous world system in which we live, even though we as Christians are not a part of it. Wealth can be used righteously for the glory of God and the good of others. How wonderful to meet someone in heaven someday who will greet you with thankfulness because the money you gave was the instrument God used in getting the gospel to him! This is what it means to make friends by means of the wealth of unrighteousness.

The parable also teaches the principle that a person's faithfulness in the use of money is a test of dedication and usefulness in other areas of life (Luke 16:10-11).

LAYING UP TREASURES

In Matthew 6 the Lord Jesus Christ defined the principle of laying up treasures. There are only two places we do this. One is on earth, the only place known to the unsaved person. These treasures, while they may seem to be wonderful, ultimately fail, either because they melt away or because the possessor has to go away and leave them. Therefore the Lord Jesus warned:

> Do not store up for yourselves treasures on earth, where moth and rust destroy, and where thieves break in and steal (Matthew 6:19).

The Lord is not saying it's wrong to save for taking care of our needs and the needs of our dependents. Wise management of finances is a virtue. Nevertheless, even the godly man's accumulated wealth, if it is merely stored and not put into the service of God, will pass away.

James pictured the future misery of ungodly men who amass wealth through oppressing others:

> Come now, you rich, weep and howl for your miseries which are coming upon you. Your riches have rotted and your garments have become moth-eaten. Your gold and your silver have rusted; and their rust will be a witness against you and will consume your flesh like fire. It is in the last days that you have stored up your treasure! (James 5:1-3)

Here is a vivid picture of wealth unused for good purposes. The corrosion of unused wealth, which could have been used in the service of God and man, stands as an accusing witness against its owners.

Any person who makes earthly wealth his only goal will fail to find lasting happiness. No matter how much we have, we always want more. How many people have ruined their lives running after wealth!

"NOT RICH TOWARD GOD"

Another parable of the Lord Jesus shows the ironic plight of the man who heaps up treasures on earth. It concerns the rich man who had so many crops that he ran out of storage space. To make room for the surplus he planned to tear down his barns and build larger ones. He supposed that, then, all would be well.

> And I will say to my soul, "Soul, you have many goods laid up for many years to come; take your ease, eat, drink and be merry" (Luke 12:19).

There is no indication that this man was a wicked person. Probably he was not. No doubt he had worked hard to amass his earthly possessions. But he had overlooked the most important thing: he was prepared for earth's tomorrow but had not given any thought at all to any tomorrow elsewhere.

> But God said to him, "You fool! This very night your soul is required of you; and now who will own what you have prepared?" (Luke 12:20).

The point of the parable is expressed by the Lord Jesus in these words:

> So is the man who stores up treasure for himself, and is not rich toward God (Luke 12:21).

Earthly riches, the object of so much concern and effort, can become utterly meaningless in an instant of time. How much more important it is to be "rich toward God"!

After telling the parable the Lord Jesus went on to show that the believer should not be anxious about the necessities of earthly life. The Lord Jesus does not condemn careful planning, but He forbids worrying. God is able to provide the food, clothing, and shelter we need.

Our attention should be fixed primarily on what is lasting. Paul, as our example, did not look "at the things which are seen, but at the things which are not seen; for the things which are seen are temporal, but the things which are not seen are eternal" (2 Corinthians 4:18).

We who know the Lord Jesus Christ should have insight that will make us different from unbelievers around us.

"For all these things the nations of the world eagerly seek; but your Father knows that you need these things. But seek His kingdom, and these things will be added to you" (Luke 12:30-31).

"TREASURES IN HEAVEN"

We are not to lay up for ourselves treasures on earth, but there is another place to lay up treasures for oneself, a place not known at all to the unbeliever, and a place all too dim for many a Christian. The only place where treasure can be laid up and really guaranteed against loss is in heaven in the presence of God. The Lord Jesus said:

> But store up for yourselves treasures in heaven, where neither moth nor rust destroys, and where thieves do not break in or steal; for where your treasure is, there your heart will be also (Matthew 6:20-21).

The Christian has been saved by the grace of God on the basis of Christ's shed blood, but how is he going to live his life for the Lord Jesus? Where is his heart?

Paul exhorted the Colossians to "keep seeking the things above, where Christ is, seated at the right hand of God" (Colossians 3:1). The believer has a heavenly salvation, a heavenly calling, a heavenly destiny, and a heavenly citizenship. How strange then and how ironic it would be to find him wrapped up completely in the things of earth! Paul continued, "Set your mind on the things above, not on the things that are on earth" (Colossians 3:2).

The believer's state or condition ought to measure up to his exalted standing in that he is complete in the Lord Jesus Christ—identified with Christ, not only in His death, but also in His glorious resurrection.

> Only conduct yourselves in a manner worthy of the gospel of Christ (Philippians 1:27).

> Walk in a manner worthy of the calling with which you have been called (Ephesians 4:1).

The stewardship of money helps to test the reality and depth of our Christian experience. We may say that we have our minds fixed on heavenly things, but we can hardly expect others to believe us if our actions prove that our greatest concern is to get ahead in the world. We are brought face to face with reality by the reminder of the Lord Jesus, "Where your treasure is, there your heart will be also."

9

STEWARDSHIP OF BODY AND MIND

◆ ◆ ◆

Scripture exhorts the believer to present his body to God. It teaches him that he is to recognize his stewardship in the possession and use of both body and mind.

> Therefore I urge you . . . to present your bodies a living and holy sacrifice, acceptable to God, which is your spiritual service of worship (Romans 12:1).

THE BODY: A STEWARDSHIP

Some philosophies of this world play down the value of the body; some glorify it and give it too much attention. The Bible emphasizes the value and sanctity of the human body and the importance of using it for God.

> For we must all appear before the judgment seat of Christ, so that each one may be recompensed for his deeds *in the body*, according to what he has done, whether good or bad (2 Corinthians 5:10).

Like the Old Testament priest who had the blood of the sacrifice applied to the tip of his right ear, the thumb of his right hand, and the big toe of his right foot (Leviticus 8:23-24), the believer has been set apart to the service of God. In effect, he says, "My ears have been redeemed by the blood of Christ to hear the word of the

Lord. My hands have been redeemed by the blood of Christ to do the work of the Lord. My feet have been redeemed by the blood of Christ to walk in the way of the Lord."

However, as no one can do anything apart from his body, we often use our bodies as instruments of sin.

In Romans 6 Paul says to believers,

> Do not go on presenting the members of your body to sin as instruments of unrighteousness; but present yourselves to God as those alive from the dead, and your members as instruments of righteousness to God. (Romans 6:13)

In 1 Corinthians 6:13-20 the apostle showed how the body is used by unsaved people (and tragically, sometimes by believers) for immoral purposes.

> Food is for the stomach and the stomach is for food, but God will do away with both of them. Yet the body is not for immorality, but for the Lord, and the Lord is for the body. Now God has not only raised the Lord, but will also raise us up through His power. Do you not know that your bodies are members of Christ? Shall I then take away the members of Christ and make them members of a prostitute? May it never be! Or do you not know that the one who joins himself to a prostitute is one body with her? For He says, "the two shall become one flesh." But the one who joins himself to the Lord is one spirit with Him. Flee immorality. Every other sin that a man commits is outside the body, but the immoral man sins against his own body. Or do you not know that your body is a temple of the Holy Spirit who is in you, whom you have from God, and that you are not your own? For you have been bought with a price: therefore glorify God in your body.

A temple is a dwelling place of God. In Old Testament times, God commanded the nation of Israel to build a temple which was the visible meeting place of God and His people. There the sacrifices were offered, and toward that place prayer was made (see 1 Kings 8:27-30). God dealt with His people through ceremonies and signs.

In the New Testament the *church* is a temple—not a building of wood and stone, but a sanctuary of living stones.

> You, as living stones, are being built up as a spiritual house, for a holy priesthood, to offer up spiritual sacrifices acceptable to God through Jesus Christ (1 Peter 2:4-5).

> So then you are no longer strangers and aliens, but you are fellow citizens with the saints, and are of God's household, having been built on the foundation of the apostles and prophets, Christ Jesus Himself being the corner stone, in whom the whole building, being fitted together, is growing into a holy temple in the Lord, in whom you also are being built together into a dwelling of God in the Spirit (Ephesians 2:19-22).

> Do you not know that you are a temple of God and that the Spirit of God dwells in you? (1 Corinthians 3:16)

Not only is the entire church a temple of God but the body of each believer is such a temple. God the Holy Spirit dwells in every Christian. Since God is holy, His dwelling place should be holy. No defilement should enter. The fact that I am living in the presence of God, and that His Holy Spirit is in some way involved in every use I make of my body, should move me to live a godly life.

> For this is the will of God, your sanctification; that is, that you abstain from sexual immorality; that each of you know how to possess his own vessel in sanctification and honor, not in lustful passion, like the Gentiles who do not know God; and that no man transgress and defraud his brother in the matter because the Lord is the avenger in all these things, just as we also told you before and solemnly warned you. For God has not called us for the purpose of impurity, but in sanctification (1 Thessalonians 4:3-7).

In addition to immoral purposes, the body is also abused through the addiction of harmful substances such as drugs, alcohol, smoking, chewing tobacco, etc. Such substances destroy the handiwork of God's creation and hinder the person from effective service. As Christians, we should exercise regularly and keep our bodies in good condition. Doing so demonstrates self-control and a willingness to be a faithful steward of the body and mind given to us by God.

THE MIND: A STEWARDSHIP

The unsaved person is subject not only to the desires of the flesh, but also of the mind (Ephesians 2:3). The Christian is not immune to either of these lines of temptation, but he has a new nature and the empowerment of the Holy Spirit to overcome temptation.

Sometimes, even when we can recognize the wickedness of our fleshly desires, we are unaware of the sinfulness of the desires of the mind. It is the tendency of the human heart to be lifted up with pride and to scorn any restraint from God. Scripture contains many warnings against pride.

> Everyone who is proud in heart is an abomination to the LORD (Proverbs 16:5).

> And all of you, clothe yourselves with humility toward one another, for God is opposed to the proud, but gives grace to the humble (1 Peter 5:5).

The Lord Jesus revealed the capacity of the human mind for evil when He said:

> "But the things that proceed out of the mouth come from the heart, and those defile the man" (Matthew 15:18).

The believer has received a renewed mind from God. By exposing himself to the teachings of the Bible his thought patterns are changed, so that he has a new attitude toward God, his environment, and himself. Yet there is a constant temptation to set one's "mind on earthly things" (Philippians 3:19). We are exhorted to set our minds "on the things above, not on the things that are on earth" (Colossians 3:2). The mind fixed on Jesus Christ is freed from chains that would keep it from reaching its highest capacity. The apostle Paul's goal was to bring his mind into complete subjection to the Lord Jesus Christ:

> We are destroying speculations and every lofty thing raised up against the knowledge of God, and we are taking every

thought captive to the obedience of Christ (2 Corinthians 10:5).

We are to use our renewed minds, yielded to the indwelling Holy Spirit, for the glory of our Savior. The mind is indeed a stewardship. If we allow our minds to dwell on those things which are unclean and unworthy, we shall bring dishonor to the Lord Jesus and shame to ourselves. The only way to avoid the wrong use of the mind is to persist in the right use of it, for the mind is never a blank tablet.

> Finally, brethren, whatever is true, whatever is honorable, whatever is right, whatever is pure, whatever is lovely, whatever is of good repute, if there is any excellence and if anything worthy of praise, dwell on these things (Philippians 4:8).

THE STEWARDSHIP OF TALENTS

In His Olivet discourse, delivered to the disciples as representatives of the nation of Israel shortly before His death, the Lord Jesus told the parable of the talents (Matthew 25:14-30). In the parable the word *talent* refers to a sum of money. The word *talent*, in modern English usage, has come to mean a "gift" or one's "natural ability." The parable has apparently influenced this usage, since the principle taught is that all of our abilities are a stewardship from God. Other passages plainly declare the same truth.

> For who regards you as superior? What do you have that you did not receive? And if you did receive it, why do you boast as if you had not received it? (1 Corinthians 4:7)

> But you shall remember the LORD your God, for it is He who is giving you power to make wealth (Deuteronomy 8:18).

> But by the grace of God I am what I am (1 Corinthians 15:10).

What God gives us is to be used for His glory. The man who was given five talents made five more talents; the man who was given two talents gained two more talents. They improved the opportunities they had. Undoubtedly many Christians are working at less than their capacity; they have not begun to develop their potential for God. When we think of financiers and captains of industry who literally wear themselves out to amass earthly fortunes and to gain earthly prestige, when we see how hard men and women work to get elected to office in the governments of this world, how weak our efforts for Christ sometimes appear! A hymn writer asked, "Must I be carried to the skies on flowery beds of ease?" Some of us answer an unqualified and shameless "yes" when we ought to respond with a plain and determined "no."

HIS COMMENDATION OF FAITHFULNESS

What the Lord especially commends in the case of the two servants with the five talents and the two talents respectively is their faithfulness.

> "Well done, good and faithful slave. You were faithful with a few things, I will put you in charge of many things; enter into the joy of your master" (Matthew 25:21).

Note that the master said the same thing to the two-talent man that he said to the five-talent man. The amount involved was not the issue; Faithfulness was the issue. "It is required of stewards that one be found trustworthy" (1 Corinthians 4:2).

Faithfulness relates to the here and the now. Some of us may think that if we had more money we would be better stewards for the Lord. Or if we were in some other place or had some other capabilities, we would serve Him better. But the man who is unfaithful with a hundred dollars will most likely also be unfaithful with a million. The man who does not serve the Lord in his own country will not likely be faithful to serve Him across the ocean. Faithfulness is tested in the little things.

> He who is faithful in a very little thing is faithful also in much; and he who is unrighteous in a very little thing is unrighteous also in much (Luke 16:10).

Faithfulness is not an abstract ideal; it is a patient, careful, continuous attention to every detail. Perhaps the reason the Lord has not given us greater funds to administer and larger opportunities for service is that He knows He cannot trust us with "much."

Our responsibility then is to be faithful with what we have now. We are not to be like the one-talent man who blamed the master for his own failure. God's justice may seem strange to some, but it is justice nevertheless.

> For to everyone who has, more shall be given, and he will have an abundance; but from the one who does not have, even what he does have shall be taken away (Matthew 25:29).

Jim Elliot, one of the martyrs among the Aucas, said, "He is no fool who gives what he cannot keep to gain what he cannot lose."

CHAPTER **10**

STEWARDSHIP OF TIME, SPEECH, AND ACTION

◆ ◆ ◆

The yielded Christian, having accepted that he completely belongs to the Lord, looks for ways to live out that principle in every area of life.

ACCOUNTABILITY FOR TIME

Another implication of stewardship is the proper use of time. The eternal God is the author of time. It is to Him we are responsible for what we do with it. David said to God, "My times are in Your hand" (Psalm 31:15). In considering his accountability to God for time, one is to reckon on the present. The past cannot be undone (although past sins can be forgiven through Jesus Christ) and we cannot control the future, but we can act in the present.

God instructs His children that they are to make the most of time. "The time has been shortened," Paul admonished (1 Corinthians 7:29). We are urged to redeem the time "because the days are evil" (Ephesians 5:16). We are to buy up every opportunity to serve the Lord Jesus Christ.

There are many different uses of time, and there must be in the life of every Christian times of recreation, relaxation, and rest, even some times of doing nothing. But such periods are to be for a purpose. There is no place for wasting time if we are to give the best account of our stewardship. We often err by spending too much time on things that may be good in themselves but which keep us from doing the better or the best.

We should not tell other Christians how to spend their time and we should avoid judging them, because that would be unscriptural. How the Christian uses his time is between him and his Lord. God may not direct another person to use his time in the same way He directs me. Many years ago some Christians probably criticized Alexander Cruden for spending so much time listing all the occurrences of all the different words in the English Bible. Some may have said he ought to have been out preaching and witnessing, winning souls to Christ instead. Think, however, of the marvelous help *Cruden's Concordance* has been to multitudes of Christians in getting to know the Bible and in becoming prepared for all kinds of Christian service.

Moses prayed, "So teach us to number our days, that we may present to You a heart of wisdom" (Psalm 90:12). Each day for the believer is a time of opportunity, a time of challenge.

> Do this, knowing the time, that it is already the hour for you to awaken from sleep; for now salvation is nearer to us than when we believed. The night is almost gone, and the day is near. Therefore let us lay aside the deeds of darkness and put on the armor of light (Romans 13:11-12).

There is no going back for the Christian, but he can go forward joyfully and triumphantly as he puts his total dependence on the Lord Jesus Christ.

ACCOUNTABILITY FOR SPEECH

We are also accountable to God for our words. The Lord Jesus Christ, before He ascended to heaven, commissioned His disciples to be His witnesses.

> But you will receive power when the Holy Spirit has come upon you; and you shall be My witnesses both in Jerusalem, and in all Judea and Samaria, and even to the remotest part of the earth (Acts 1:8).

Witnessing is the responsibility of every child of God. Not all have the same field of service, not all have the same breadth of opportunity, but all are to be witnesses. We have the responsibility of being faithful in the place where God has put us.

The early Christians went everywhere preaching the Word. In their daily occupations, no matter what the conditions and circumstances, they made Christ known. A mere word, of course, not backed up by godly Christian living, may be of little force; but if we do not let our light shine before men, how can they glorify our Father who is in heaven, since they cannot see Him and do not know Him? (Matthew 5:16).

Our speech, then, is indeed a sacred stewardship. We have been entrusted with the gospel, not only for ourselves, but also for the eternal benefit of others.

> How then will they call on Him in whom they have not believed? How will they believe in Him whom they have not heard? And how will they hear without a preacher? How will they preach unless they are sent? Just as it is written, "How beautiful are the feet of those who bring good news of good things!" (Romans 10:14-15).

> So faith comes from hearing, and hearing by the [spoken] word of Christ (Romans 10:17).

May we be like the disciples of old, who, when they were commanded to be silent, boldly replied, "For we cannot stop speaking about what we have seen and heard" (Acts 4:20).

SOUND SPEECH

Not only are we stewards of speech to say the right thing for the Lord, but we should also be careful not to say the wrong thing. Often in Scripture we are warned against rash words.

The believer is exhorted to be "sound in speech which is beyond reproach" (Titus 2:8). James told us that the tongue's capacity for evil is boundless. We sin by inciting others to sin—directly by such sins as lying and blasphemy, and indirectly by applauding the sins of others.

And the tongue is a fire, the very world of iniquity; the tongue is set among our members as that which defiles the entire body, and sets on fire the course of our life, and is set on fire by hell (James 3:6).

Scripture repeatedly warns us against lying, evil speaking, and other sins of speech.

Therefore, laying aside falsehood, speak truth each one of you with his neighbor, for we are members of one another (Ephesians 4:25).

Do not lie to one another, since you laid aside the old self with its evil practices (Colossians 3:9).

Let no unwholesome word proceed from your mouth, but only such a word as is good for edification according to the need of the moment, so that it will give grace to those who hear (Ephesians 4:29).

As we become increasingly aware of our stewardship of speech, we can pray from the heart: "Set a guard, O LORD, over my mouth; Keep watch over the door of my lips" (Psalm 141:3). When we yield our speech to Him we become an occasion of praise to our Lord instead of a stumbling block to others, and what we say will exemplify this beautiful description:

Like apples of gold in settings of silver is a word spoken in right circumstances (Proverbs 25:11).

ACCOUNTABILITY FOR ACTION

Stewardship concerns the whole of life. It involves doing the will of God in thought, word, and deed.

Doing the will of God is a part of our stewardship because we really don't belong to ourselves. Our lives have been entrusted to us to use for Him to whom we really belong.

For the love of Christ controls us, having concluded this, that one died for all, therefore all died; and He died for all, so that they who live might no longer live for themselves, but for Him who died and rose again on their behalf (2 Corinthians 5:14-15).

Surely every Christian wants to do the will of God! Many are confused, however, about God's will. How can we know what the will of God is for us when there are so many possible roads to take, so many different decisions to be made day after day after day? We cannot expect that He will speak to us miraculously with an audible voice or give us some unusual sign, because He has already spoken and has given us His word in written form. The Bible is where we discover the will of God.

A principle we find throughout the Bible concerning the discovery of God's will is that He makes His will known to those who obey Him. Do we really want to know the will of God for us? *Then we must obey what we already know to be His will.* We are responsible to obey what we have learned from the Bible about God's will for our stewardship.

> Therefore, to one who knows the right thing to do and does not do it, to him it is sin (James 4:17).

We see this in the life of Abraham:

> By faith Abraham, when he was called, obeyed by going out to a place which he was to receive for an inheritance; and he went out, not knowing where he was going (Hebrews 11:8).

Abraham did not know where he was going, but he knew the God who had called him to go.

"THE WILL OF GOD IN CHRIST JESUS"

If we really want to be good stewards, we should search the Scriptures with the definite intention of finding those statements which declare the will of God and then proceed to act upon them. Obedience is the prerequisite to discovery.

There are many passages of Scripture that declare the will of God and have a direct bearing on our stewardship. For example:

Rejoice always; pray without ceasing; in everything give thanks; for this is God's will for you in Christ Jesus (1 Thessalonians 5:16-18).

"Rejoice always." The joy of the Lord is quite different from the happiness of the world, which depends on circumstances. This joy is a gift from God. Because He is unchanging and unchangeable, joy can be constant, even when mingled with affliction and heaviness of heart. Joy can be manifested in the exercise of our stewardship.

The Macedonian Christians were exceedingly joyful in their liberality. To respond to life joyfully is certainly the will of God for me. But if I face life glumly, how can I expect my heavenly Father to reveal further aspects of His will, since I am not obeying what I already know to be His will? I should not be surprised to be left in darkness, since I have rejected the light He has given.

If you want to be a rejoicing, trusting steward, "In everything give thanks; for this is God's will for you in Christ Jesus" (1 Thessalonians 5:18). The unhappy, complaining Christian is obviously not doing all the will of God that he knows. Like the murmuring Israelites in the wilderness he will miss out on much of God's blessing.

> They quickly forgot His works;
> They did not wait for His counsel,
> But craved intensely in the wilderness,
> And tempted God in the desert.
> So He gave them their request,
> But sent a wasting disease among them.
> (Psalm 106:13-15).

The Christian life is—or ought to be—a life of thanksgiving. The will of God is the best thing for any of us. Since He has made His will known in these and many other particulars, it is essential for us to obey if we want to be counted faithful in total stewardship.

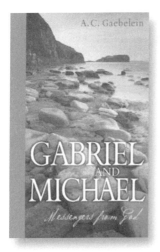
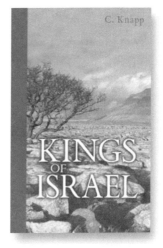
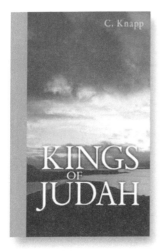
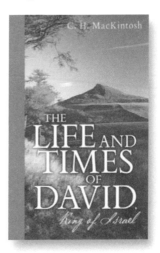

THE FOUNDATION SERIES

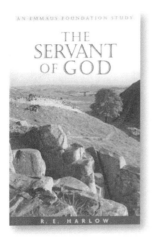

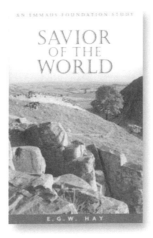

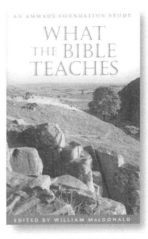

The Servant of God

Savior of the World

What the Bible Teaches

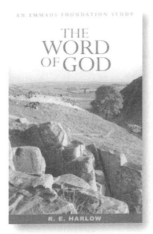

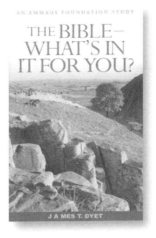

The Word of God

The Bible — What's In It For You?

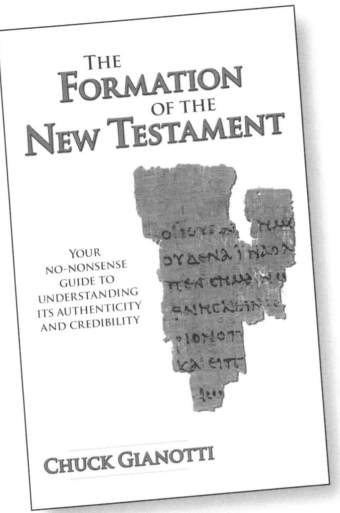

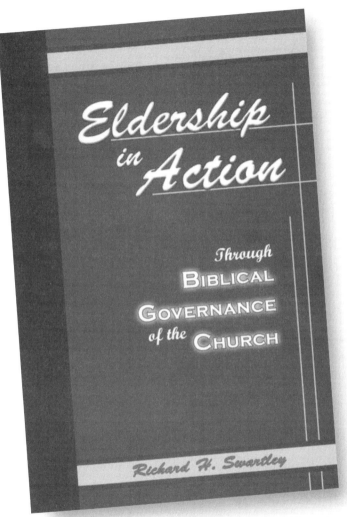

**Eldership in Action: Through
Biblical Governance of the Church**